Kings of the Road

Kings of the Road

How Frank Shorter, Bill Rodgers,
and Alberto Salazar
Made Running Go Boom

Cameron Stracher

Houghton Mifflin Harcourt
Boston • New York
2013

Library of Congress Cataloging-in-Publication Data is available.
ISBN 978-0-547-77396-4

Book design by Brian Moore

Printed in the United States of America
DOC 10 9 8 7 6 5 4 3 2 1

For Dr. Robert J. Kim and Dr. Richard Lange,
who kept me running

Contents

Where does the power come from, to see the race to its end?
From within.

— ERIC LIDDELL, *CHARIOTS OF FIRE*

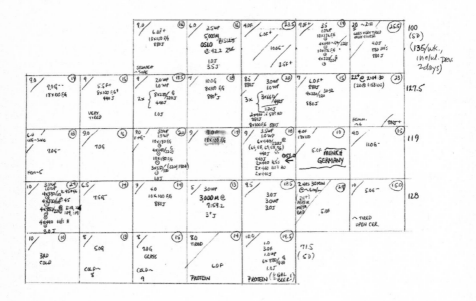

Training log kept by Jack Bacheler of his workouts with Frank Shorter in the
month before the Munich Olympics.

Courtesy Jack Bacheler

Preface

The race is not to the swift. It is, instead, to the resolute and implacable, the steadfast, unswerving, and devoted. Any fool can dash down a straightaway and collapse in a heap. But to continue when every nerve in the body is screaming to stop, to push past fatigue, exhaustion, and despair, to ignore reason and embrace the irrational. That is true greatness. The mark of a champion.

During the decade from 1972 to 1982, three American men became world champions in the sport of distance running. They rose from obscurity and raced their way into the country's hearts and minds. Their victories were celebrated on the front pages of newspapers, heralded on magazine covers, and trumpeted by television commentators. They became household names, and their accomplishments spurred millions to join them. In their footsteps, running boomed, and an industry worth billions was born.

Frank Shorter, Bill Rodgers, and Alberto Salazar did not set out to be heroes for a generation weary of war and unrest. Each wanted, simply, to be the best in the world. They overcame barriers erected by others and proved to themselves they had the strength, willpower, and leg speed to win. Not for fame or fortune — amateur rules at the time prohibited them from earning a dime — but for the pure love of the sport.

Shorter was the trailblazer, the doctor's son from Connecticut who dropped out of medical school to pursue his dream. Yale educated, raised in upper-middle-class comfort, he harbored a dark family secret that pushed him to run harder, faster, and farther in a futile effort to keep it at bay. Self-coached, he experimented with training at altitude and on the track, running 440-yard intervals with a miler's precision. He was fiercely loyal to friends such as Steve Prefontaine, but he also could be aloof and secretive, and he wasn't beyond playing mind games with his competitors before or during a big race. His breakthrough at the Munich Olympics would light the torch for everything that followed.

Bill Rodgers, his contemporary, graduated from Wesleyan University and wandered aimlessly astride his motorcycle with a pack of cigarettes in the last years of the Vietnam War. A conscientious objector, he returned to running because it was all he had left during those dark and empty days. He survived on food stamps, while he ran hundreds of laps indoors on an old wooden track when it was too cold to run outside in the Boston winter. The Greater Boston Track Club would provide him with teammates and a home, and with them he put together a life that exploded into public view one Monday in April.

Alberto Salazar was "the Rookie," the high school phenomenon who trained with Rodgers as a skinny, awkward sixteen-year-old. His father had fought beside Fidel Castro and Che Guevara in the Cuban Revolution, then fled to the United States when Castro turned Cuba into a godless republic. The boy inherited his father's hotheadedness and ran both to please the man and to escape him. Nothing stopped him: not fatigue, heat, or even death. He was determined to be the world record holder — before his twenty-second birthday.

Each runner discovered his ability in an almost accidental way, and each progressed on a path without clear guideposts. There was no organized state program to develop their promise, no nutritionists and trainers to monitor their every twitch, no corporate interests to underwrite their training. They ran because they had to, transforming the sport in the United States and dominating the world for most of a decade.

Since that time, no American man has attained their level of achievement, and only Joan Benoit Samuelson (during roughly the same time period) achieved their name recognition. Indeed, since their heyday, no U.S. runner (with the exception of Samuelson in 1984 and Bruce Bickford in 1985) has won a gold medal in any Olympic event or been ranked first in the world at any distance longer than 400 meters.

Was it something in the air? Something in the water? Some magic pixie dust that turned the United States from a country of pot-smoking hippies to a nation of fleet-footed runners? Suddenly, skinny guys were cool, and LSD was an acronym for "long slow distance." Grown men appeared on the roads in their long underwear and gloves, battling traffic for the shoulder. Swooshes and stripes became tribal commitments, while gel, goo, and goop became breakfast.

Their deeds, however, might have been doomed to oblivion, vanished in the margins of *Obscure Sports Quarterly*, except for one thing: they had one another. In that gloomy decade, they came to prominence in the glow of one another's achievements. Shorter-Rodgers-Salazar. Trailblazer-Popularizer-Usurper. Brains-Soul-Heart. Their competition made them train harder, race faster, strategize better. By themselves, they might have simply won races; together, they changed everything.

The marathon would establish them, and the track would distinguish them, but it was on the roads at the non-marathon distances where they made their greatest impression. The road race was the prime showcase for their prolific talents. The track was too special-

ized and the marathon too intimidating, but a road race was something the average person could love. An untrained novice could toe
the line with the best in the world, standing shoulder to shoulder
until the gun went off. He could jump into a five-mile race on a
Saturday morning and still have plenty of time for breakfast and a
nap. It was a people's event led by world-class athletes, the perfect
venue for the children of the revolution who had turned inward to
self-improvement. Yet in an increasingly complex and confusing
world, running was also a commitment to something larger than
the self: the road race as collective achievement, where everyone
was a "winner." Shorter, Rodgers, and Salazar led the way, and in
their wake a thousand races bloomed.

Of all the races born during this decade, one stood apart. One
race ruled them all. It began as a small midweek jaunt in a nonde-
script Cape Cod town, organized as an excuse to go barhopping, and
it blossomed into an international sporting event, drawing the elite
to its starting line. It became the proving ground for everyone who
was anyone and quickly gained the reputation as the best road race
in the United States. In the course of ten years, Shorter, Rodgers,
and Salazar dominated, winning seven times, setting seven course
records, and making the town their home.

The Falmouth Road Race was the perfect metaphor for the running boom. It was birthed by Shorter, nurtured by Rodgers, and
reached its apogee with Salazar. It was also the first, last, and only
race where the three men competed head-to-head. The story of
Falmouth is the story of running during its golden age, its rise and
growth mirroring America's love affair with the sport. It is also a
story about the United States at a time when one moment was ending and another beginning. In the depths of a spiritual and economic crisis, a renaissance was stirring — in the cities, in the arts,
in business and finance. Running was both a symptom of Sisyphean
despair and the antidote to discontent and torpor. One foot in front
of the other, a meaningless activity, and yet the most profound.

Falmouth was the measure of a runner's conviction and the place to which he returned, to race against others and himself.

This story, then, begins and ends in Falmouth. But it starts in the middle, in 1978, when a brash young upstart tried to run his elder off the road, and nearly died trying.

Bill Rodgers and Alberto Salazar battle it out on the beach in the 1978 Falmouth Road Race.

Courtesy Charlie Rodgers

1

Duo in the Sun (1978)

I've never met a runner who didn't think he could run faster.

— RUDY CHAPA

T HE HAND-DRAWN SIGN was taped to the wall over his bed, a reminder of failure and an exhortation against defeat: YOU WILL NEVER BE BROKEN AGAIN. After his disastrous sixth-place finish in the 10,000 meters at the NCAA finals, he swore he would not be out-trained or outraced again. He was no longer "the Rookie," the skinny kid from Wayland High School who trained with the big boys from the Greater Boston Track Club on the Boston College track. Alberto Salazar had just completed his sophomore year at the University of Oregon, chasing the promise of his high school potential. His frame had filled out, and his arms flexed with new biceps and triceps. He was tall, good-looking, and olive-skinned, with a thick swatch of hair on his chest and head. The son of Cuban émigrés — his family had fled to the United States when he was two years old — he was a prodigy, heralded for his speed as much as his work ethic and fierce competitiveness.

But now he was trailing his mentor and former teammate, Bill

Rodgers, after four and a half miles. Rodgers was the people's champion, the face of American distance running. Fans along the road called out to "Boston Billy," cheering him on. Frank Shorter was the Olympic champion, yet it was Rodgers who carried the torch. If Shorter was the past, Rodgers was the present. Alberto Salazar, however, was the future.

So he pulled up alongside Rodgers. The sun beat down on both runners. The temperature was a deceptive 78 degrees, the humidity 70 percent. They had run the last mile, a straight shot along the beach, at a 4:30 pace. Now the heat had taken its toll. Both runners were drenched in sweat, their shirts clinging to their chests, their nylon shorts chafing their thighs. They doused themselves with water at every opportunity, but it made little difference with the humidity. Nothing evaporated in the thick ocean air. There was no respite; there was only the road.

Salazar turned to Rodgers and asked if the older man wanted him to take the pace. It was an old ploy to dishearten a rival. Let him think you felt so fresh you would willingly set the pace. And it worked. "Take it. It's yours," said Rodgers.

Alberto Salazar put the hammer down to take the lead on the roads at the height of the running boom. The future, he thought, was now.

On the morning of August 21, 1978, four thousand runners flooded the streets of Woods Hole, Massachusetts, for the sixth annual Falmouth Road Race. A seven-mile run from the Captain Kidd bar to the Brothers Four tavern in Falmouth Heights, the race was the brainchild of Brothers Four bartender Tommy Leonard. It had become so popular that the field of four thousand runners filled up nineteen days after registration opened, and yet six hundred more crashed the race and ran unofficially. The list of registered runners read like a Who's Who of American road racing. Thirteen sub-four milers; sixteen NCAA or AAU champions; nine Olympians. There was Garry Bjorklund, the Olympic 10,000-meter finalist; Mike

Roche, winner of the Peachtree Road Race and an Olympic steeple-chaser; Craig Virgin, the AAU 10,000-meter champion, who had flown in from Brussels for the race; and Alberto Salazar, the previous year's runner-up. On the women's side, course record holder Kim Merritt was back to defend her title against Boston Marathon winner Gayle Barron, 10,000-meter road record holder Martha White, and Joan Benoit, who had won the 1976 race as a Bowdoin college sophomore.

Topping the list, however, was Bill Rodgers. Rodgers was coming off a string of victories at the marathons in New York, Boston, and Fukuoka, Japan, making him the only runner ever to hold the title of all three races at the same time. He had set course records at Boston and New York and was also the course record holder at Falmouth. Although Falmouth's shorter distance would seem to favor the 10,000-meter runners (10,000 meters is about 6.2 miles), no one underestimated Boston Billy. On the roads, Rodgers could push a punishing pace, surging on the downhills and breaking his competitors. The only way to beat him, according to conventional wisdom, was to try to stick close and then outkick him. If it came down to a sprint, Rodgers was most vulnerable. His fastest mile was only 4:18, a pedestrian time that even a good high school miler could beat. Of course, Rodgers had no intention of letting anyone stay close enough to outkick him.

By 7 a.m., the air was already moist with humidity. A slight breeze off the water provided little relief. In the distance, a ferry horn sounded a sonorous bleat. It was still three hours to race time, but Woods Hole looked like a town prepared for a foreign occupation. Red barrier fencing lined Water Street from the post office all the way down to the aquarium. Porta-Johns clustered in rows of tens and twenties in the Marine Biological Laboratory parking lot, near the Swope dormitory, and along Church Street. Traffic cones demarcated starting zones, and a police cruiser with flashing lights blocked passage over the town's drawbridge.

At the crest of the first hill, where Water Street merged into Route

28 and ferry traffic bound for Martha's Vineyard funneled into the Steamship Authority, a group of volunteers in bright RACE OFFICIAL T-shirts gathered with local police to talk strategy. The Town of Falmouth had forced race organizers to limit the field this year because of the narrow start and the crush of runners at the finish. But organizers worried about "bandits," unregistered runners who would jump into the pack after the race began—hence the barrier fencing. The fencing was only a partial solution, however; it couldn't be extended over the entire course. Indeed, beyond the library, where the fencing ended, several runners without numbers were already stretching.

The finish line was another problem. Because of crowd control, this year it had been shifted two hundred yards farther down the hill in front of a large grassy field. The idea was to funnel the runners through longer chutes and avoid the backup onto the course. But recording the times of four thousand runners was a logistical nightmare. In the days before personal computers, barcodes, and radio frequency devices, this involved matching runners' numbers on their racing bibs with an electronic printout of their times as they crossed the finish line. If a single runner was missed, it screwed up the entire count. In that case, according to a local newspaper, a volunteer with a high-tech device known as a tape recorder would "stand at the end of the shoot [sic] and say the numbers of runners into the tape."

There were dozens of other problems—large and small—associated with planning and pulling off an event with thousands of participants and tens of thousands of spectators. At that time, there were very few races bigger than Falmouth—Peachtree had more runners, but the Boston Marathon had fewer—and except for the expanded finish area, the course was just two lanes wide.

The most serious problem race organizers had to face, however, was the heat. Legend has it that the first "marathoner"—the Greek messenger Pheidippides—ran from Marathon to Athens to announce the Athenians' victory over the Persians at the Battle of

Marathon. Then he promptly dropped dead. Falmouth was not the rocky, sun-bleached terrain of Greece, but the race started later than most, and it was exceptionally humid, which impeded the body's ability to cool itself.

If Salazar wasn't worried about the heat, he should have been. The race began at 10 a.m. in the middle of the hottest month on Cape Cod. The slowest runners would not finish until high noon. Dr. Arthur Robinson, the medical director of the race, had expressed his concerns to the local paper. His daughter, Nancy, had been a track star at Falmouth High School and was dating Salazar. The couple met in high school while racing on the Massachusetts track circuit. Everyone knew the boy wonder from Wayland, with his dark eyes and invincible aura. What was a little heat to such a phenom? Something to generate, dissipate in waves off his brown shoulders, roil the girls (and their mothers) on the sidelines.

Around 7:30 a.m., the buses started to arrive. Falmouth was a point-to-point course, like the Boston and New York City Marathons, but there was no room in Woods Hole for four thousand cars. Instead, race organizers closed Route 28 and provided free transportation to the start. The buses dropped runners at the top of School Street and, except for the elite and sub-elite, they had to walk about half a mile around Eel Pond to the starting line. The drugstore was still open, as was the small grocery store, but by 8:30 it was too difficult to enter the latter, and the former was packed with runners buying last-minute items such as Vaseline (to prevent chafing) and Band-Aids (to prevent men's nipples from bleeding). The smell of Ben-Gay was strong in the aisles as several runners unabashedly rubbed down their calves and thighs. Local residents fought their way through the throng to buy the morning *Boston Globe* and *New York Times*. A couple grumbled about the crowds and the smell, but most knew someone who was running, had run themselves, or simply felt lifted by the spectacle.

It was hard not to be inspired by the sight of thousands of fit, healthy, athletic bodies. Muscled legs, flat bellies, taut arms. Men and women stripped down to shorts and tank tops, lightweight clothing and shoes made especially for running by Dolfin, Tiger, and Etonic, as well as by new companies owned by Rodgers and Frank Shorter. The race was a competition, but it was also a social event. The runners chatted amiably as they soaked up the camaraderie, energized by their common goal and their moment in the sun.

The elite runners arrived in Woods Hole less than thirty minutes before the race began. Each had his own routine, but they all shared certain similarities: a warm-up, a massage, stretching, then some sprints up and down Water Street. Nothing too fast, but enough to get the legs loose to avoid cramping or tears during the early part of the race. They gathered in the parking lot behind the main building of the Woods Hole Oceanographic Institution, seeking the only shade around. For the first time, the race had a corporate sponsor — Perrier, the French mineral water company — which kicked in the whopping sum of $5,000. But there was no prize money for the winners, and some elite runners had to pay their own travel costs. Falmouth families hosted many of them, and although this was a charming tradition, it had grown out of economic necessity: the race simply could not afford to pay the travel costs of all but a handful.

Spectators sitting on the stone wall in front of the post office shouted good luck to Rodgers, and every few minutes another runner came up to shake his hand. It was distracting, and even a little annoying, but Rodgers handled it all with good cheer. He waved to the crowd and accepted their good wishes like the captain of the football team. When he spoke, he sounded as if he had just taken a hit of really good weed, the kind that makes you wide-eyed and amiable. His sudden fame was still strange to him, and he moved among his fans in a kind of winsome daze.

Salazar, however, remained aloof from the fray. He stretched by himself and said little to anyone. Some mistook this for arrogance, and, in truth, he was supremely self-confident. His coach, Bill Dellinger, said he was "obsessed with being the best in the world."

The editor in chief of *Runner's World* called him "the fiercest, most combative runner I've ever met." He had been a star for so long, a prodigy on the track and the roads, that his self-confidence was well earned and rarely challenged. But his intensity also masked profound insecurity. The son of a dogmatic and strict, religious father, and the youngest of three brothers, Salazar could be painfully shy. He took failure hard in a sport where finishing second and losing were rarely distinguishable, and the sting of his NCAA sixth-place finish was still fresh and raw. Even when he won, he seemed to derive little joy in victory. *Not losing* was more important than winning.

Despite their differences, the two men shared certain characteristics common among distance runners: asceticism, introversion, neurosis. You could not run mile after mile at a sub-five-minute pace without a bizarre dedication to self-abnegation. Even now, distance running has yet to produce the equivalent of Usain Bolt parading around the stadium with his finger in the air. Instead, runners tend to save their celebrations for the bar after the award ceremony.

The first three miles from Woods Hole to Falmouth favored the distance runner. With its tight start, twisting roads, and short, quick hills, most participants were exhausted before the race opened up on Surf Drive. Then it was a flat mile in the hot sun, followed by five turns before heading back up a small hill toward Falmouth Heights. If Rodgers could not shake his pursuers by the time the runners got to Surf Drive, it was anybody's race. Speed would be tested against endurance; legs measured against heart.

Now they lined up at the start, shoulder to shoulder, as the crowd pressed in. Spectators stood on the roofs of Fishmonger's and the Captain Kidd. All along Water Street, people pressed three or four deep against the barrier fencing. In the sky, helicopters buzzed, news crews jockeying for the best position. Latecomers were still hustling down the street, but race volunteers were closing it down. Linking arms, they walked in lockstep toward the starting line, funneling everyone across the drawbridge. A man with the wrong bib tried to get through, and a race volunteer barked at him: *Seeded runners only. Everyone else around the block.* He shuffled off sheepishly like a truant schoolboy.

Salazar found a place at the front, one spot away from Mike Roche. Several former Boston teammates tucked in near him. Rodgers, however, was two rows back, content to let the speedsters set the early pace. A man with a megaphone was telling everyone to move back, make room for the top seeds. They were not quite behind the starting line, and the race would not be official until they were. There was some pushing, and more exhortations from the man with the megaphone, and the runners moved back a couple of feet. Sweaty bodies wedged against sweaty bodies, with nowhere to go in the crush.

Finally, with a few more shoves, everyone was behind the line. The helicopters thrummed overhead. A police escort flashed its lights, clearing the road with a whoop from its siren. The press truck gunned its engine, belching diesel and soot. A tape recording crackled over the loudspeakers, and the runners stood at attention as "The Star-Spangled Banner" played. There were flags everywhere, and necks craned in different directions like supplicants praying to different gods. Then the megaphone man gave final instructions and hurried back to the pace car. The starter raised his pistol. Legs tensed; arms raised; breath held. The race was about to begin.

When the gun sounded, the field surged out of Woods Hole like a crazy centipede. The lead runners were over the bridge and up the hill in a straight shot, but it took ten minutes for the rest of the field to get over the line, and even longer before they could run at a comfortable pace. The front pack quickly established itself. There were always a few kids who went out too fast — either for the glory or from sheer ignorance — and the experienced runners let them go. The adrenaline of the start, and the way the hill quickly leveled off and then descended all the way to the first mile mark, made for unwise decisions. But because no one had a clear view of the leaders on the winding road, the elite athletes would let them go only so far; losing the thread in the early stages of a race was a tactical blunder.

They hit the first mile in 4:25. It was almost unbearably picturesque: Nobska Lighthouse in the foreground, a rocky bluff overlooking Vineyard Sound, a snaking tail of runners stretching back as far as the eye could see. Two helicopters hovered above the bluff, and a flotilla of boats bobbed just off the beach. It felt like a festival, or a carnival, except up at the front some of the best runners in the world battled for position. They were all business as they took the hill and then descended back into the woods.

The second mile passed in 8:49, on pace for a course record. No one was thinking record, however; they were just trying to hold the thread. On this part of the course, there were two short hills followed by a longer one: up, down; up, down; up, down. It was shaded, but the trees held in the humidity, and the road felt slippery and damp. Spectators edged onto Oyster Pond Road, offering sponges, orange slices, cups of water. These were scientists and their families, who lived in the summer cottages nestled in the woods and spent several months doing research at the Marine Biological Laboratory before returning to their winter homes. There was an official water stop in another half mile, but the runners were grateful for the aid. The lead pack passed without breaking stride, but several runners in the next group snatched at the cups, knocking them from the hands of inexperienced volunteers but managing to grab a replacement. They doused their heads with water, took a couple of sips, and then tossed the empty cup onto the road.

Rodgers surged on the downhills, forcing the others to keep pace. It was just the way he ran, almost unconsciously, but it broke the rhythm of his pursuers. They were running his race, and every time he moved, they had no choice but to respond. His strategy was to run the first three miles hard, ease back over the next three, and do what he had to at the finish. He knew the course and how to attack it, and that was also to his advantage. He knew what to

9

expect on the other side of every hill — how long the downslope lasted and how hard he could push. None of the others in the lead pack knew the course as well, and some were seeing it for the first time. Unlike the track, where every lap was uniform and flat, the road offered constant surprises. For runners without a mental picture of what came next, the hills and turns were not only physically demanding but also psychologically devastating. As the legs tired, the mind needed a distraction, a promise that the pain would soon end. But without knowing what lay ahead, runners could easily become discouraged. Their competitors played tricks on them, sprinting when they actually had nothing left, hoping to break the spirit when the body couldn't follow. The longer the distance, the greater the ploy.

Salazar had a different advantage: the ability to endure great pain. He did not consider himself fast, but since elementary school he had been able to push through oxygen depletion, soft-tissue injury, viral infections. It was as if the biochemical pathways that trigger the body's warning systems didn't work for him. Indeed, there is some scientific research suggesting that certain people are more immune to the signals of pain. How much of Salazar's imperviousness was pure genetics, how much mental rigor? It's a question that probably can never be answered. But when Rodgers surged, Salazar surged with him, playing a game of "me and my shadow." For a while, it seemed as if there was nothing Rodgers could do that would dispirit the Rookie. Salazar dogged his every step, keeping the older man in his sights.

The heat increased; the humidity thickened; the sun blazed gold in the silver sky. Winged and swift, a thing of beauty unfolded.

The year 1978 was a time of great change and transition in the United States, a fulcrum between 1960s liberalism and a growing conservative backlash. That summer was the compliance deadline for Title IX, requiring gender equality in collegiate athletics. But in the spring, the U.S. Supreme Court in *Regents of the University of*

California v. Bakke drove a nail in the coffin of affirmative action, ruling that UC Davis's policy of setting aside a number of admissions slots for disadvantaged students constituted "reverse discrimination." Disco ruled the pop charts, with three songs from the soundtrack of *Saturday Night Fever* climbing to number one. But the new wave group Blondie released *Parallel Lines,* which would go on to sell more than twenty million copies. Meanwhile, the seminal punk band, the Sex Pistols, played its last show, and later that year Sid Vicious would be arrested for murdering his girlfriend, Nancy Spungen. Prince, Van Halen, and the Police released their debut albums, while musicians such as the Ramones, Talking Heads, and Elvis Costello dominated the underground. In theaters, the first mainstream and commercial movie to deal with the Vietnam War, *The Deer Hunter,* won Oscars for best picture, best director, and best supporting actor (for the young Christopher Walken). But in case anyone might conclude that Americans had turned serious and introspective, *Animal House* and *Halloween* were also released to great popularity.

It was not exactly the best of times, nor the worst of times, but a sense of unease and displacement haunted a younger generation that couldn't identify with Woodstock and saw a future of diminished influence and economic expectations. Their parents had fled the cities, leaving them empty and divided, while the suburbs were blank and soulless. In the years to come, the sixties would fade into the go-go eighties, hippie love replaced by junk bonds and "morning in America." But in 1978, the nation seemed to be at war with itself, an inner turmoil rather than the explosive conflict of the Vietnam era. On the surface, disco balls glittered, yet beneath the glitz punk rock seethed.

The road, however, was narrow and true, with none of the ambiguity of color, class, or culture. The clock reckoned time in tenth-of-a-second increments, and the finish line was clearly marked. In the end, the best man won.

• • •

On Surf Drive, the course opened up to a mile-and-a-half straight-away. The runners came down a short hill, around a salt marsh, and there was the beach — sparkling and lethal. The lead pack of ten men had dwindled to four: Salazar, Rodgers, Craig Virgin, and Mike Roche. Despite the jockeying in the hills, this was where the race would begin. The temperature had risen a few degrees, and the sun burned white through the haze. There was a slight wind at their backs, but not enough to help, and certainly not enough to cool them.

Roche and Rodgers ran side by side, with Virgin and Salazar one half-step behind. Roche was confident. He had gone to the front at the very beginning, fighting for the lead in the first 800 meters. But that was a crucial mistake. His early burst of speed was taking its toll. Rodgers surged again, and Roche could not respond.

Neither could Virgin. He had set personal records nine times over the past month in Europe. He was an excellent runner, with the best natural leg speed in the group. The distance was ideal, right in his sweet spot, but the mental and physical toll of trying to keep pace with the surging Rodgers, coupled with the long overseas flight, exhausted him. He had tried to run a controlled race, but that had been difficult on the twisting first half of the unfamiliar course against top competition. Now he simply concluded he could not keep pace. Within about sixty seconds, Rodgers had a fifteen-yard lead on him.

Only Salazar didn't yield. Like the other runners, lactic acid had built up in his muscles, and his heart was working harder, trying to supply the oxygen that his body so desperately needed. But it was his brain that would decide when to slow down, a decision it would make only after it had evaluated all the physical data and concluded it was in the body's best interest. Unless they ripped or tore, muscles did not stop on their own. They obeyed the brain's command. Salazar's brain made his knees lift, his calves flex, his thighs extend. His muscles burned, but his brain told them to keep going: *You will never be broken again.*

12

Of course, Rodgers didn't know what Salazar's brain was saying. His own brain was telling him he had managed to shake two pursuers, but one still doggedly tailed him. Worse, that pursuer was the heralded star from the University of Oregon whom Rodgers himself had anointed the future king. The race was heading into its final stages, and if Rodgers couldn't shake Salazar within the next mile or so, he had little hope of being able to outsprint him. For the first time, doubts about his ability to win this race and hold his title crept into his head. He could feel Salazar beside him, matching him stride for stride as they approached the far end of Surf Drive.

It was then that Salazar asked if Rodgers wanted him to take the pace. For Rodgers, it was the final blow. He was done. The race was Salazar's. "Take it. It's yours," he said.

But that was the last he saw of the runner. Rather than pulling in front, Salazar began to wobble like a car whose driver has died at the wheel. Roche passed him. Then Virgin passed him. Spectators watched him weave across the road as he dropped to fifth place, then sixth, seventh, eighth. There was something seriously wrong, but no one knew how to respond. He was literally losing consciousness as his legs motored him forward. His brain could no longer tell his body what to do.

Up ahead, Rodgers was lengthening his lead. With his last challenger gone, he coasted easily past the marina and made his final turn toward the ball field. He acknowledged the crowd with a quick smile and a wave of his hand. Victory was sweet, but sweeter still was the knowledge that he was still the king.

Somehow Salazar managed to make the final hill in Falmouth Heights, but as he crossed the finish line, he collapsed. They carried him to the medical tent, where his core body temperature was measured at 108 degrees. Medical personnel worked furiously to revive him. They dumped him in ice water to cool him down. His father showed up, hotheaded and panicked. Runners continued to cross the finish line, but Alberto Salazar lay semiconscious in a plastic tub filled with ice, moaning, thrashing, and cursing. His brain was simply another body part, fallible and weak. He had failed, and he lay broken in defeat.

Now a priest touched his forehead. His father gripped his hand. The young athlete hovered on the knife-edge of darkness. At the height of the running boom, it appeared, the future had ended before it began.

Frank Shorter winning America's first gold medal in
the Olympic marathon in sixty-four years.

Getty Images

2

Birth of the Boom (1972)

Running helped me discover how I wanted to live. It gave me the
feeling like I had finished and accomplished something.

— FRANK SHORTER

THE TERRORISTS ARRIVED before dawn. Dressed in red
training suits and carrying duffel bags, they hopped a fence
with the help of several American athletes. Security was lax,
and no one bothered to ask questions or stop them. These were
the "Friendly Games," the Germans' attempt to make people forget the last Olympics held in Berlin, in 1936, before Hitler's approv-
ing glare. Climbing a fence in the early morning after a night of
drinking seemed just the thing to do. Now the eight Palestinians,
members of the Black September group, moved stealthily toward
31 Connollystrasse, where athletes from Uruguay, Hong Kong, and
Israel were housed. It was 4:10 a.m. on September 5, 1972.

At the first apartment, they kicked in the door, waking Yossef
Gutfreund, an Israeli wrestling referee. He threw himself against the
frame and shouted for his countrymen to escape. Tuvia Sokolovsky,
a weightlifting coach, managed to break a window and flee, but the

other five coaches and referees were not as lucky. They were captured, tied up, and brought with Gutfreund to an empty second-floor bedroom as hostages.

The terrorists then forced wrestling coach Moshe Weinberg to lead them to the rest of his teammates. Weinberg calculated that the wrestlers and weightlifters would stand a better chance of overpowering his captors, so he convinced them that apartment two, which housed the Israeli marksmen, fencers, and track-and-field athletes, was occupied by the Uruguayan team. They moved on, instead, to apartment three, where one wrestler broke free, but his remaining teammates were seized. When Weinberg and weightlifter Yossef Romano tried to escape, they were shot and killed.

Weinberg's body fell to the pavement, where a security guard found him and alerted German authorities. Thus began a twenty-one-hour ordeal that ended when West German police botched a rescue operation at the airport after the terrorists arrived there by helicopter, expecting to be flown to Cairo to continue negotiations. In the ensuing firefight, the terrorists killed the remaining hostages. When it was over, eleven athletes, five terrorists, and one policeman were dead.

The American distance runner Frank Shorter watched the terror unfold from his balcony directly across the way from the Israeli compound. He had gone to sleep that night with the reassuring word that the athletes were safe. In the morning, he awoke to the grim truth. Up until that time, the Munich Olympics had been a huge success. Four hundred companies and 6,000 workers had labored six years at a cost of $850 million to build the stadiums and village. One hundred twenty-two countries sent 7,000 athletes to the games; 1.2 million spectators attended in the first six days; 7,000 reporters were a constant presence; and 800 million people watched the opening ceremonies live on television. It was, as the terrorists knew, the biggest stage in the world on which to be watched. The Olympics made a star out of swimmer Mark Spitz and a petite gymnast named Olga Korbut. The Swedish swimmer Gunnar Larsson beat the American Tim McKee in the 400-meter medley in a photo finish that required stretching the swimmers' times to three decimal places to determine the victor. The U.S. basketball team lost the gold medal to the Soviets for the first time in twenty-eight years, in what some have called "the most controversial game in international basketball history," a game marred by officiating errors. And Dave Wottle, in his signature golf cap, won a thrilling victory in the 800 meters, coming from dead last in the final two hundred meters to win by three-hundredths of a second.

But now as Shorter and his teammates Kenny Moore and Jack Bacheler wondered what would happen to their event — the marathon — the politicians debated whether to let the Olympics continue. Israeli prime minister Golda Meir called for the games' cancellation, as did the influential *New York Times* sports columnist Red Smith. At the opposite extreme, Arab nations boycotted the memorial ceremony for the slain athletes. Letting the games continue seemed disrespectful and futile. How could running give meaning to murder? And yet not to run seemed equally meaningless. Nothing would bring back the dead.

Shorter did his best to stay prepared for the marathon. He had already run the 10,000 meters (finishing fifth), and he was tired and tight from the race. Trying to stay loose, he jogged around the confines of the village with Moore and Bacheler. He was not a politician, and he could not rewrite history. All he could do was run.

He was a doctor's son from New England, a headstrong boy who had his own ideas about what he wanted to do. He had been a skier but turned to running when he read that the French ski team was beating the Austrians because the French ran in the off-season. He convinced his gym teacher to let him jog by himself around the field while the other kids played football. Soon he was running to school as well, two miles in low-cut Keds, a book tucked beneath his arm.

It was at the private Mount Hermon School in Northfield, Massachusetts, that he ran his first Pie Race, an annual 4.55-mile road race in which all the men who finished under thirty-three minutes and all the women who finished under forty minutes got an apple pie. In a field of runners mostly older and better trained, he finished seventh, picking off people in the second half of the race and discovering that he had speed in addition to endurance. It wasn't until his junior year, however, that he joined the cross-country team, and even then he was ambivalent about his commitment to the sport. But in the fall of 1964, during his final year at Mount Hermon, he was undefeated in cross-country and broke every record on the courses he ran, winning the New England championships as well as the Pie Race. He quit the ski team and in the spring track season set a school record in the two-mile run, while continuing his unbeaten streak.

He went on to Yale, where running came second to his premed studies and his grades. He didn't want to commit to something if he couldn't see a clear path to success. Like his father, he was a toiler and a puritan, who frowned on frivolity. But from his mother he inherited a romantic side. It was a love of the unknown and untried that led him to attempt his first marathon during the summer between his junior and senior years. The race just happened to be the U.S. Olympic trials in Alamosa, Colorado, and it drew the best runners in the country. Not used to the distance, the altitude (6,800 feet), or the heat, and with borrowed shoes that were a half size too small, he dropped out at fifteen miles. But the race showed him what it took to run with the best.

He returned to Yale, torn between his romantic and pragmatic sides. To help resolve the conflict, he sought the advice of his coach, Bob Giegengack. Shorter wanted to know how good he could be. Giegengack, who had coached the 1964 Olympic team and was one of the top track coaches in the country, responded, "If you train hard and make a commitment, you could probably make the Olympic team."

It was what Shorter needed to hear. During spring break, he started running double workouts and increased his distance to eighty miles a week. With graduation upon him, he set his sights on the national collegiate outdoor championships in Knoxville, Tennessee. In the six-mile (the equivalent of 10,000 meters), he won by thirty-two seconds, and he finished second in the three-mile by only one second. With those two races, Shorter announced himself as one of the most promising distance runners in the United States.

But he still had to eat. Being a professional distance runner was no career for a Yalie. In 1968, in fact, it was no career for anyone. There were no shoe contracts, no prize money for winning races, and no corporate sponsors to fund training, travel, and housing. Instead, succumbing to his practical side, Shorter went to New Mexico, where his parents had relocated, and enrolled in medical school at the state university in Albuquerque.

By day, he studied and attended classes. At night and before dawn, he ran. This lasted six weeks. He dropped out of school when the administration would not let him modify his academic schedule so that he could run. His decision was a triumph of passion over reason, yet it was also quite rational. He was a good runner, maybe a great one. To give up running now, without seeing how far he could take his talent, would, in his mind, be irrational. Medical school could wait; his best years as a runner would not.

So Shorter moved in with his parents in Taos and helped them finish construction of their house. When he wasn't working, he ran along the back roads and dirt paths of the impoverished town. A skinny white guy, no taller than five foot nine, was an easy target, and Shorter attracted the interest of a group of pachucos, or small-town thugs, who chased him through the streets. After that, when he went running, his father followed him in his pickup, a .38 by his side. Once, when the pachucos approached, his father fired several shots above their heads to scare them away. They never bothered Shorter again.

He ran aimlessly, twelve to fifteen miles a day, wherever his legs took him. But after seven months on his own, he realized he wasn't going to get any faster by running alone. He reached out to Jack

Bacheler, who had beaten him in the two-mile at the Florida Relays. Bacheler was living in Gainesville, where he was pursuing a graduate degree in entomology while continuing his running. Shorter invited himself down, and soon the two young men were training with a small group of runners in the Florida Track Club.

The FTC had been founded in 1965 by the University of Florida's track coach, Jimmy Carnes. It was, at first, a means for transfer students to compete while they waited to become officially eligible for the college team. Bacheler became the first noncollegian to join the team while he attended graduate school. Not long after that, Jeff Galloway, who was in a master's program at Florida State University, and John Parker, who was getting his law degree, signed up. They were soon joined by miler Marty Liquori, who was ranked number one in the world in the 1500 meters. Although Gainesville is not an ideal place to run — too hot, too humid — it became a mecca for middle-distance and long-distance running, a hub of the running boom along with two other weather-challenged cities: Boston, Massachusetts, and Eugene, Oregon.

Shorter roomed with Parker, who would go on to write the best-selling novel *Once a Runner.* At Parker's urging, Shorter enrolled in law school. At $2.40 per credit each quarter, even an impoverished runner could afford it.

In June 1970, Shorter won both the three-mile and six-mile at the AAU championships. As a result, he was invited to compete against the Russians in Leningrad at the annual U.S.-Soviet dual meet. He won the 10,000 meters, and his upset victory earned him a spot on the cover of *Sports Illustrated,* a rare honor for a distance runner. The second-place finisher was University of Oregon graduate Kenny Moore. Moore and Shorter would become close friends, and it was Moore who convinced him to move up to the marathon. Later, Moore would claim (in jest) that the only reason he'd suggested that Shorter run the marathon was so that he, Moore, could beat him.

A year later, Moore did beat Shorter in the marathon at the AAU championships in Eugene. It would be the last time. In August, at the Pan American Games, Shorter won his first marathon, as well as the 10,000 meters. In December, against some of the world's best, he won the prestigious Fukuoka Marathon in Japan and shaved five minutes off his personal best time.

Suddenly, Frank Shorter was the number-one-ranked marathoner in the world. Barely known in his own country, he was nevertheless the United States' best hope for an Olympic medal in an event no American had won for sixty-four years.

At the end of May 1972, Shorter moved from Gainesville to Vail, Colorado, to train at altitude with Bacheler and Galloway. They ran twice, sometimes three times, a day for twenty miles or more. Shorter slept ten hours a night, with a nap squeezed in between runs. Their workouts were intense, all the more remarkable because they did them at altitude, where the air is thinner, with less oxygen. On June 1, they ran sixteen quarter-miles, each between sixty and sixty-four seconds, with less than thirty seconds of rest between them. At that pace, Shorter was running close to the equivalent of four 4-minute miles in a single workout. They ran thirty-two 220-yard sprints with an impossibly short recovery (around fifteen seconds). Shorter trained for the marathon as if he were running track, and simply increased the number of intervals and decreased the recovery time. He was one of the first marathoners to realize that over the course of twenty-six miles, speed is almost as important for victory as endurance, and he would use his ability to run intervals to devastating advantage.

At the U.S. Olympic trials, Shorter ran both the 10,000 meters and the marathon. The first three finishers in each event would be selected for the team, with runners-up selected as alternates. The process was brutal, unforgiving, and capricious. A bad race, an injury, a cold, or a spill on the track, and an athlete would be shut out of the games. If Shorter made the team, he would have to run two first-class marathons within two months, which increased the risk of burnout and injury. Yet in the 10,000 meters, in 95-degree heat, he went out fast and never looked back. In the marathon, he and Kenny Moore took an early lead, and they stuck together to finish tied for first. Bacheler claimed the third spot, easing past Jeff Galloway, who had already made the team in the 10,000.

Now the three friends and teammates waited patiently in the Olympic Village to hear whether the event for which they had trained so hard would be canceled. It was hard not to feel selfish at a moment like this, and yet no good would come from thinking of themselves. As Moore put it later, they had been living in a refuge, immune "from a larger, seedier world in which individuals and governments refused to adhere to any humane code." But that world had intruded in Munich, rejecting the artificial boundaries the athletes had constructed, and painted everything in the somber tones of death.

When International Olympic Committee chairman Avery Brundage announced that the games would continue, those in attendance at Olympic Stadium cheered, but Israel sent the rest of its team home in protest. Mark Spitz, with his seven gold medals, returned to the United States for his own protection. Other Jewish athletes were given a security detail. Armed police patrolled the village like an occupied territory, and overnight the Friendly Games became the deadly games.

As a result of the services for the slain athletes, the marathon was rescheduled from September 9 to September 10, the final day of track-and-field events. Although the British favorite, Ron Hill, complained about the change and later claimed that it ruined his chance for a medal, it worked to Shorter's advantage, giving him an extra day's rest after his two 10,000-meter races. The terrorist attacks also increased press coverage of subsequent events and focused the world's attention on the marathon. As ABC anchor Jim McKay noted, the beginning of the marathon marked a "change of mood" in Olympic Stadium, as spectators "put sadness aside" for the first time since the murders. Thus, in a cruel bit of irony, the Munich massacre set the stage for a compelling narrative of resurrection, redemption, and victory. The network couldn't have asked for a better story line for the American television audience.

The marathon was an odd event, with little traction in the United States at the time. Now at 26 miles, 385 yards, the length was not even fixed until 1921. In the first seven Olympic marathons, runners covered six different distances, ranging from about 24 miles to 27 miles, with the course changing to accommodate local topography, historical happenstance, and the British royal family (in order to give them a better view). The United States had a champion in Johnny Hayes, who won a controversial race in 1908, when the Italian runner Dorando Pietri took a wrong turn entering Olympic Stadium, collapsed, and was half carried across the finish line by officials. The United States filed a protest, and Pietri was disqualified, giving the gold medal to Hayes.

But it had been a sixty-four-year drought since Hayes's victory. In fact, during that time the United States had been shut out at all distances above the mile, except for victories in the 5000 and 10,000 meters in 1964. The athletic culture of the country, with its emphasis on football, baseball, and basketball, created sprinters but not distance runners. It was easy enough for a football star to run track in the off-season, but there were few places for the distance runner beyond the lonely confines of the roads. The United States had high hopes in these games for Shorter's friend and teammate Steve Prefontaine, famous for his aggressive front running, good looks, and charismatic personality. But after taking the lead in the 5000, Prefontaine had faltered over the final 150 meters and ended up missing a medal by one place.

Now it all came down to Shorter. Although he was ranked number one in the world, the oddsmakers favored Hill, who had run 2:10 at Boston, shattering the course record by three minutes, and the Australian Derek Clayton, who held the world record of 2:08:33. Neither thought much of Shorter. Clayton believed that Shorter's leg action was "too high," and Hill thought he would be worn-out from racing the 10,000 meters. In anticipation of a competitive race,

ABC had cameras placed all along the course. In addition to McKay, the network hired novelist Erich Segal, of *Love Story* fame, to provide color commentary. Segal had been Shorter's classics professor at Yale and was an amateur marathoner, but he had no experience as an announcer, as would soon become apparent.

The race began at 3 p.m. The day broke warm and humid, which again favored Shorter, who was accustomed to the heat and humidity of Gainesville. The course followed the outline of the Olympic mascot, a dachshund named Waldi, with runners starting at the back of the dog's neck, then proceeding through mostly flat, shady residential neighborhoods and parks. In the second half of the race, there was a long, twisting stretch of gravel road that runners had complained about in the days leading up to the race because of its loose footing. Then the course made its way back into Olympic Stadium for a final lap.

Seventy-four runners from thirty-nine countries had qualified for the marathon. Now they toed the line in front of 60,000 spectators in the stadium. A race official gave the runners final instructions, then hustled to the side of the track. The starter raised his pistol. The small mob of athletes tensed: heads bowed, knees bent, arms frozen. Then the gun went off. The runners bolted down the straightaway and into the first turn. Although there was no advantage to jumping into the lead, few could resist the adrenaline rush and the lure of instant, albeit short-lived, glory. They completed the turn, moved into the backstretch, and headed through a tunnel that led out onto the road. Hill and Clayton took an early lead, while the other runners tried to keep them in view. Although there were plenty of miles to make up the difference, too many races were lost by failing to answer a challenge. The one thing any contender could not afford was to let these two get too far out of sight.

They hit ten kilometers at a fairly brisk 31:15. Shorter was ten seconds behind Hill and Clayton and beginning to suffer blisters from the new inserts he had placed in his Adidas racing flats earlier in the week. But he ignored the pain and at the first water station reached for a bottle marked with the radiation hazard symbol. In the bottle was Coca-Cola that he and Kenny Moore had allowed to go flat, so as to avoid stomach cramps from the carbonation. The sugar and caffeine gave him a boost, like a low-budget energy drink. He felt comfortable, his muscles relaxed and his breathing controlled.

Clayton was leading, and Shorter trailed in a small group about fifty meters behind. Just before fifteen kilometers, the pace slowed, and Shorter found himself coming up on the leaders. As he described it, he realized that if he didn't deliberately slow down, he was going to take the lead, a risky move so early in the race. He decided then and there, however, to let his momentum take him. He wrote: "I'd committed myself. This was it — the break. I told myself to get as far ahead as I could because if I got far enough ahead, I honestly thought no one would catch me. I'm not sure anyone but me considered my move a break at the time; a 5- or 10-second lead is not unusual in a marathon and certainly not much with 16 or 17 miles to go." But the warm conditions were to his liking, the split times had been reasonable, and he preferred to be in control. It was the way he had run Fukuoka and the Olympic trials: take a relatively early lead and push the pace. If anyone wanted to beat him, they would have to run his race. He threw down the gauntlet and dared the field to rise to his challenge.

At fifteen kilometers, he had five seconds on the field. By twenty-five kilometers, he was ahead by fifty-seven seconds. Now it was other runners who were losing sight of him. There was still a long way to go, but the odds kept improving with every step. In order to beat him — unless he imploded on his own — someone was going to have to pick up the pace, and soon.

At thirty kilometers, his lead continued to grow. Meanwhile, Moore had moved into second, and Bacheler was in sixth, only thirty-eight seconds behind Moore. After the sixty-four-year drought, it suddenly looked as if there might be an American flood. Shorter was running smoothly and compactly, his stride controlled, no effort showing on his face. He was practically a case study in efficient biomechanics. There was no wasted motion, no extra kinetics. Despite Clayton's biased observations, Shorter's leg lift was perfect, his body leaned forward slightly, his head held steady, and his arms swung in muscular cadence.

The crowds along the race route were three or four deep in places, and they cheered on the American runner, his white singlet with the red USA logo and his bib number, 1014, prominently displayed. A press bus belching diesel kept pace, but Shorter seemed untroubled by the fumes. He entered the English Garden with a solid lead. This was where the road turned to gravel and twisted like a mountain switchback for the next four miles. Shorter knew that if he reached the garden with a lead, it would be hard for his competitors to overcome him, as they would not be able to see him on the twisting paths. Now his strategy paid off. He not only held his lead, but he increased it to ninety seconds. Suddenly, with four and a half miles to go, he could sense victory. That sweet anticipation was glorious, the most satisfying feeling he had ever experienced. Even if it was only dopamine, it felt like ecstasy.

He focused on a singular goal: get to the stadium. The last miles were grueling, but he knew that with this lead, his competitors would have to run twenty-five seconds per mile faster to catch him, a nearly impossible task at the end of a marathon. Even if he slowed to a seven-minute pace in the last mile, he would still win. He repeated these facts to himself like a mantra, and the mantra kept his legs churning. The race was his to lose, and he didn't intend to lose it.

Up ahead was the stadium: concrete and steel in the dusk. As he approached the tunnel that led beneath it and onto the track, he heard a huge explosion of cheers. He was momentarily confused. What could it be? The high jump? A world record? But then he was inside the tunnel and cocooned in silence. It was the signature moment of the Olympic Games for him, the one he would remember for years to come: the tunnel symbolizing the end of the marathon, the link between the outside world and the finish line. The cool, dark passage leading to victory.

When he finally emerged onto the track, he heard . . . silence. That was odd, he thought, but he ignored it and began his sprint to the finish. As he did, the silence turned to catcalls and boos. It appeared that the hometown crowd was belittling the American's victory. In fact, they were protesting the removal of a German student, Norbert Sudhaus, who had jumped into the marathon right before the finish — incredible, considering the terrorist attacks and the additional security precautions taken by the Germans. With his running shorts, singlet, and muscular build, Sudhaus had fooled the crowd into thinking a German was about to win the race.

In the announcer's booth, Erich Segal shouted, "That's not Frank. That's not Frank. It's an imposter. Get that guy off the track! How can this happen at the Olympic Games? It's bush league. Get rid of that guy. There's Frank Shorter. That's Frank. Come on, Frank, you won it!" This endearingly unprofessional outburst would capture the public's imagination almost as much as Shorter's victory: a burst of raw emotion that gave voice to the competitive spirit of distance running and the passion of its devotees.

As Shorter surged around the final turn, he was spent, and nearly loopy, but still running about five minutes per mile. One hundred meters from the finish line, the boos turned to cheers, and he raised his right fist to acknowledge them, the first time during the entire race he'd allowed his concentration to waver. A few more strides, and he was across the line, a slight smile creasing his face. He dropped both arms, then drew them briefly heavenward, before placing them on his head, as if in disbelief at his accomplishment and overwhelmed by emotion.

After sixty-four years, America had itself a marathon champion. And in that instant, shadowed by death and loss, the running boom was born.

From left to right: Boston Globe sports reporter Joe Concannon,
unidentified man, Tommy Leonard, Vince Fleming, and Bill Rodgers.

Courtesy Charlie Rodgers

3

A Man. A Plan. A Road Race. (1973)

A bar at the start, and a bar at the finish. What else could you want?
— TOMMY LEONARD

TOMMY LEONARD WAS a drinker with a running problem. A bartender in Boston, he was what people affectionately called a character. He knew everyone, and everyone knew him, and if he didn't know you, once he served you a beer, you'd soon become his lifelong pal. With his stocky body, ruddy face, and big mustache, he fit no one's stereotype of the typical runner. He appeared, instead, to be one of those scrappy Irish kids who'd grown up on the TV series *The Little Rascals*. Only his skinny legs betrayed him.

He had come to running early in life. As a boy, he ran away from his first foster home, climbing through the window of the playroom and out onto Franklin Street in Westfield, Massachusetts. He was six years old, his father in failing health from a lifetime of alcoholism and his mother too poor to raise him and his sister. Over the years, he would run away from many foster homes and goodhearted but

31

unprepared families, until running was more natural than staying put.

In high school, Tommy naturally gravitated toward track and field. After finishing next to last in the 100-yard dash, however, he decided he was better suited for the distance events. Thus began a lifelong love affair with the sport of running, a sport that kept him (relatively) sober and out of trouble. He served in the marines during the Korean War, where, among his other claims to fame, he finished second in a First Naval District cross-country race in South Boston. He kept up his running after he left the service, regularly logging thirty-five to forty miles a week. It was, as he put it, "the greatest cure in the world for a hangover." In the 1960s, while everyone else was "frying their brains out" on acid and marijuana, his addiction was running.

He wasn't fast, but what he lacked in speed he made up for in stamina. Over the years, he ran twenty-six marathons, twenty-two of them in Boston. He knew how to pace himself, and he knew how to party. Some people run for the endorphins. Tommy Leonard ran for the beer. "A road race is a moving street party," he once said. "At the end of every race, there's a cold beer waiting."

He poured them himself at the Eliot Lounge, a grubby watering hole on the corner of Commonwealth and Massachusetts Avenues, close to the finish line of the Boston Marathon and just a few blocks from Fenway Park. Decorated in a style described by the *Boston Globe* as "early grandfather's attic," it was on life support when Tommy was hired in 1972, so quiet that patrons would play chess at the bar. Years later, Charles Pierce would write its obituary in *Sports Illustrated*:

Once, there was a place where nobody batted an eye the night the horse walked in. The horse stopped to visit with everyone sitting at the bar, and then it took eight people to get him out again, and nobody in the place thought it at all remarkable, though they thought the horse well-behaved. Once, there was a place where the

Stanford band marched in playing *Truckin'* and marched out playing *White Punks on Dope*. Once, there was a place where Fuzzy
Zoeller came in for a drink at the end of the day and wound up
tending bar until four in the morning . . . Once, there was a place
where a future Olympic gold-medal runner spent the night of the
Boston Marathon biting complete strangers on their hindquarters
and playing the trumpet besides.

But when Tommy arrived, the bar hadn't been put out of its mis-
ery yet. Tommy became the daytime bartender, and to this unlikely
setting, he brought his enthusiasm for running. It spilled over the
counter and lit the gloomy tavern with the warm glow of hearth and
home.

In Tommy's first year at the Eliot, he offered a free beer to everyone who ran the Boston Marathon. Because he lived near the Boston
College track, where he occasionally worked out, he naturally came
to meet and befriend the members of the Greater Boston Track
Club who ran there, too. Of course, this led to invitations to drink
at the Eliot Lounge, and soon the GBTC coach, Bill Squires, could
be happily found in an informal "coach's corner" in the bar, where
he offered free running advice to anyone who asked, while Tommy
made sure the beer flowed freely.

The Eliot Lounge became Boston's running bar, *the* place to be,
especially after the Boston Marathon. More than that, it became a
sports bar par excellence, Cheers before Cheers was Cheers. When
Red Sox pitcher Bill Lee was asked how it felt to face potential Hall
of Famer Don Gullett in the 1975 World Series, Lee quipped, "He
may be going to the Hall of Fame, but I'm going to the Eliot Lounge."
After Bill Rodgers won his first of four Boston Marathons, he told
the press, "I'm going to the Eliot Lounge to have a Blue Whale" (a
mixture of blue curaçao, vodka, gin, rum, and a couple of cherries).
Like Disney World, the Eliot Lounge was the magical destination
where winners (and losers) went to commemorate their toils and
share the joy with Tommy. As Bill Higgins wrote in the *Cape Cod*

Times, "Spend time with Tommy and you're sure to smile, unless you have no soul. The eternal optimist, his glass of Guinness is always half-full."

The Eliot was Tommy's home, but like every hard-partying Boston boy, he had a summer share on the Cape. His was the Brothers Four tavern, which overlooked Vineyard Sound from its perch in Falmouth Heights. The bar was a hangout for the college crowd that surged into the Heights during the summer months. Along with the nearby Casino-by-the-Sea, the Brothers kept the streets of Falmouth Heights hopping late into the night and the police force busy locking up drunks and trespassers urinating on homeowners' lawns.

It was at the Brothers, in the early afternoon of September 10, 1972, that Tommy had the television tuned to a sport few of his patrons were interested in watching: the Olympic marathon. The high season had ended, and the tourists were gone, but Tommy still had his regulars, and this Sunday afternoon was no exception: the few, the proud, the hungover. Regardless of their lack of interest, Tommy shut down the bar and refused to serve another beer until the race concluded. There were mild protests, but the handful of drinkers didn't really mind. Tommy was always good company, and his passion for the marathon was entertaining and contagious. He provided his own color commentary, growing more animated as the race progressed and the American Frank Shorter moved into the lead. No one else in the bar that day understood the thrill Tommy felt watching these guys plod along, mile after mile, but they had to admit it was pretty exciting to see the USA emblem on Shorter's chest. With every mile, they became even more enthusiastic as it appeared that an American was going to win the culminating event at the world's biggest athletic competition.

"How many miles?" someone asked.

"Twenty-six," someone else said.

"Twenty-six miles and three hundred eighty-five yards," Tommy corrected him.

When Shorter entered the English Garden, Tommy could barely

34

contain himself. His nerves were jangled, and he couldn't sit still. Barring an unforeseen breakdown, the United States was about to have its first gold medalist in the marathon in sixty-four years. For Tommy, it seemed as if his beloved sport was emerging triumphant along with Shorter, bursting into homes, gyms, and bars with a vibrancy as sharp as Tommy himself. Running had been his life since those early days in the foster homes, and seeing Shorter winning made him feel as if he were winning, too. Not just this race, but all that striving over the years, the running from place to place, all for this one moment.

Shorter approached the stadium, and the crowd in the bar went wild. The fans in the stadium, however, were more subdued, until Norbert Sudhaus appeared on the Munich track. Then the stands exploded. "What the heck!" said Tommy, echoing Erich Segal. The police rushed the interloper off the track, and the catcalls in the Brothers Four turned to cheers (while in the stadium the cheers turned to catcalls). Then Shorter emerged, and Tommy gripped the bar rail so tightly his fingers hurt. Lean, quick, and clean, Shorter sprinted the final three hundred meters, the smile on his face an acknowledgment of a secret he and Tommy possessed. A race could stop time, lift the spirit, bring joy to the darkest heart. A race could change the world.

When it was over, Tommy's face was red and his brow lined with perspiration, as if he had just run the marathon himself. "That was exhausting," he said. The gathered multitude had to laugh. Whether he meant to or not, Tommy always made them laugh.

Tommy chuckled along with his buddies and customers. But later that night, he would ask himself, "Wouldn't it be fantastic if we could get Frank Shorter to run a race in Falmouth?" And he made that his dream.

Despite Shorter's gold medal, the most famous runner in the United States later that year was a horse. Secretariat, a gorgeous chestnut stallion who stood sixteen hands tall, won the Triple Crown for the first time in twenty-five years. He could have easily beaten Frank Shorter in the mile, although the horse wouldn't have stood a chance against the man in the marathon.

While Secretariat romped around the track and Shorter loped along the roads, a bungled burglary at the Watergate Hotel threatened the second term of President Richard Nixon. In its wake, his top aides, H. R. Haldeman and John Ehrlichman, were forced to resign, and Nixon fired the White House counsel, John Dean. Later that year, in the "Saturday night massacre," the president dismissed independent prosecutor Archibald Cox, which prompted the resignations of Attorney General Elliot Richardson and Deputy Attorney General William Ruckelshaus. His vice president, Spiro Agnew, resigned as a result of corruption charges unrelated to Watergate, and Nixon famously declared, "I am not a crook!" which would soon prove incorrect.

That same year, the Supreme Court decided *Roe v. Wade,* affirming a woman's constitutional right to an abortion, in what may have been the high point of the court's liberal activism. In May, armed protesters occupied the town of Wounded Knee, South Dakota, to protest U.S. government treatment of Native Americans. After seventy-one days and several deaths, both sides eventually disarmed, but not before the siege attracted national attention when actor Marlon Brando sent Sacheen Littlefeather, in full Apache dress, to decline his Oscar for the *Godfather,* in protest of the treatment of Native Americans and their depiction in Hollywood films.

Overseas, the United States finally ended its overt military involvement in Vietnam, although it would be two more years before North Vietnam captured Saigon and the war officially concluded. For his role in establishing a cease-fire, U.S. secretary of state Henry Kissinger was awarded the Nobel Peace Prize, which sparked public outrage and led to the resignation of two members of the Nobel Committee. On Yom Kippur, Syria and Egypt attacked Israel, punching a hole in the Jewish nation's aura of military superiority, which had existed since its victory in the Six-Day War in 1967. As a result of U.S. support and military assistance to Israel, OPEC cut off oil supplies to the United States, leading to the first (but not the last) spike in gasoline prices and forever changing the balance of power in the Middle East.

Yet in this political and economic maelstrom, the arts flourished. Thomas Pynchon published his masterpiece *Gravity's Rainbow;* a young writer named Toni Morrison published her second novel, *Sula,* which was nominated for a National Book Award; and Kurt Vonnegut published *Breakfast of Champions.* Directors Martin Scorsese and George Lucas announced their arrival on the scene with the films *Mean Streets* and *American Graffiti,* while the punk music club CBGB opened in New York's East Village, ushering in a prolific period of musical experimentation.

And on the roads, a quiet revolution had begun, birthed by men who were not revolutionaries and, later, by women who were. To outsiders, it appeared they were running away from the future. But in fact, they were running toward it.

Guy Fuller Field, behind the recreation center in the middle of Falmouth, had exactly one tree. That was where Lucia Carroll sat on a bench watching her husband, John, train Tammy Hennemuth, who had qualified for the Junior Olympics in the 440-yard dash. It was hot, the tree offered little shade, and the cinder track on which Tammy ran coughed up black dust with every stride she took.

John had discovered Tammy one day during her freshman year as she walked across the high school field. She looked athletic and played hockey, basketball, and tennis. Her brother ran track, but she had never given it a second thought. "Hey!" John called out to her. "You want to run cross-country?" No one had ever recruited her before, and she was intrigued. But mostly she wanted to get out of Confirmation class, so she agreed.

She soon learned that being coached by John was serious business. Before each race, the team evaluated the competition and talked about race strategy and pacing. Afterward, there were meetings to discuss the highlights and to analyze their mistakes and weaknesses. John gave each girl on the team a training program that he personalized and closely monitored. They used their weekend races to log more training — running five or six events on a Saturday — in order to peak for the bigger meets, such as the nationals and the AAU championships. They did everything except watch game-day films, and that was only because John lacked the budget to hire a cameraman.

John Carroll was a three-time state high school champion in the 800 meters. Barrel-chested, strong-armed, and thick of thigh, he was built for the race: pure speed and tenacity, with the winner the guy who could gut it out the longest. He went to Boston College on a track scholarship and had a successful, albeit unremarkable, collegiate career. After graduating, he traveled to Baghdad, where he taught English to Iraqi students for two years at a private Jesuit high school.

The track, however, stayed in his blood. He loved the feeling of speed, the acceleration off the turn, spikes slapping on cinders, an elbow in the ribs. While in Europe, he spent time with Will Cloney, the legendary director of the Boston Marathon, who was managing the U.S. track-and-field team. He met Olympians such as Billy Mills and Tom Farrell, while also watching European women training on the track and in the parks, something he had never seen before in the United States. That short experience would have a profound effect on him.

Upon his return to the States, he got a part-time coaching job at a public school in Hartford, Connecticut, where he met a young brunette named Lucia Bonaiuto. They married a year later. In the fall of 1971, the couple moved to Falmouth, where John taught high school English and coached track, and Lucia worked in a variety of office positions. Track, however, meant *boys'* track, because there was no girls' program at Falmouth High School. The administration could not fathom that young girls would voluntarily submit to the rigors of running around an oval, and no one wanted to be responsible for the physical damage it might do to their muscles, bones, and ovaries.

John wasn't looking for trouble, but he had seen women run in Europe and knew they were as competitive, committed, and enthusiastic about running as men. He also knew they were fast. What happened next followed more from his love of the sport than from any feminist leaning.

The following fall, he recruited twelve girls to run cross-country. The next season, he had thirty. Over resistance from the administration, he made the girls work out with the boys' track teams and race indoors as well as outdoors. He found meets for them in faraway places, sometimes driving six or seven hours to compete. The girls studied and slept on the back seats and floor of his VW van. Although there were few races for women longer than 800 meters (the Olympics did not even have a women's mile until 1972), he made them run long distances, and even had his sprinters run cross-country. He ran with them, and when they fell back, he told them they could drop out, which only made them more determined to keep up. After practice, he drove them home, which often made him late for his own dinner. When they traveled to races in the New York area, they stayed at Lucia's parents' house in Connecticut, and she cooked a hot meal for the team. He took them to the Armory in Washington Heights, Manhattan, and told them to keep their elbows out to avoid getting pushed off the old wooden track. When they fell, he helped them remove the splinters from their knees.

Within a few years, he had a coterie of competitive athletes. They had no idea how good they could be until John pushed them. Johanna Forman won the high school girls' indoor national mile and ran the third-fastest juniors' time ever on the Van Cortlandt course in New York. Tammy Hennemuth was on the mile relay team that broke the national girls' high school record. Nancy Robinson qualified for and ran the 440-yard dash at the nationals. They competed against women who would become the superstars of U.S. running: Judi St. Hilaire, Joan Benoit, Lynn Jennings. They never doubted themselves, because John told them they were capable of anything. He believed it, and they believed it, and the lessons they learned stayed with them throughout their lives.

Lucia was proud of her husband and proud of the efforts he took to make his girls succeed. She knew he didn't coddle them. He trained them like professional athletes, harder and longer than they had ever experienced, and they responded. Tammy Hennemuth, for example, lacked the raw talent of Johanna Forman, but she was a workhorse. Whatever John asked of her, she would do, and more. She had guts and determination, and she took a loss as a reason to push herself harder. John cultivated those values — he knew that winning required more than good genes — and he urged the girls to do one more mile, one more interval, one more race.

The big sweaty guy who sat down next to Lucia on the bench was impressed, too. He wanted to know if that was her husband out there, training the girl. Lucia said it was, and bragged to him about Tammy's achievements. Talk of the Junior Olympics got Tommy Leonard started about Shorter's victory in the Munich Olympics. He told Lucia he wanted to organize a marathon, from Woods Hole to Falmouth, door-to-door from the Captain Kidd to the Brothers Four.

"That's hardly a marathon," Lucia observed.

"I don't know how to plan something like that," said Tommy, for whom the numbers didn't really matter. "Do you think your husband could help?"

Despite the sweat pouring off his brow and his red face and cheeks, Tommy appeared harmless, like one of Santa's elves who had gotten trapped on an exercise bicycle. And a road race would be nothing for John, who had organized all-day track meets with seven hundred screaming high school kids. Sure, she said, committing her husband to the dream of this garrulous man.

After the workout, Lucia introduced the two men. Tommy talked about Shorter's victory as if he were still watching it. Now he wanted to do something for the kids in Falmouth: their own road race to inspire them. John thought it would be a good way to raise money for the girls' track team. Or maybe that was Tommy's idea — later, no one could remember for certain. They agreed that John would recruit track team members to help with the registration and logistics, and Tommy would spread the word to the running community outside Falmouth. The two men shook hands, with no idea what they had just gotten themselves into.

The road race as sport and drinking excuse has a long and not always illustrious history. The oldest-known footraces took place in Sumer starting in about 2035 BC. They were run by couriers and were followed by animal sacrifices. The Greek Olympic Games began in 776 BC with a single 200-meter race. By 720 BC, a 400-meter race had been added, as well as a distance race of about three miles. The marathon, despite its origins in Greek history, was never run at the ancient Olympics. Races were run barefoot and naked, which probably led to their decline among the more prudish Romans, who viewed running for anything other than military training as a waste of effort.

In the *Iliad,* Homer describes the first account of someone psyching out a competitor during a race: "The son of Peleus then offered prizes for speed in running . . . [Ajax] took the lead at once . . . Close behind him was Ulysses — treading in his footprints before the dust could settle there, and Ajax could feel his breath on the back of his head as he ran swiftly on." Distracted, Ajax slipped on cow dung and lost the race.

In the Middle Ages, footraces were a large part of various festivals. There were sack races and wheelbarrow races, as well as races for Jews, old men, and prostitutes. In the late eighteenth and early nineteenth centuries, aristocrats began wagering on how quickly their footmen could cover certain long distances, either by running or racewalking. Soon the working classes picked up the sport, which became known as "pedestrianism." A few noted pedestrians, such as Captain Robert Barclay Allardice, actively trained for contests. In

1808, Captain Barclay covered one thousand miles in one thousand hours, walking one mile every hour and sleeping no more than one and a half hours at any given time for nearly forty-one days. Barclay had a famous competitor in Abraham Wood, who, according to running historian Edward Sears, once bet that he could "catch a duck on the turnpike road, pluck it, roast it, eat it, then run a five minute mile." He won the bet, running a 4:56 mile and washing down the duck with a quart of ale.

Barclay's training methods were cataloged by Walter Thom in the oldest-known book on running, published in 1813. According to Thom, a pedestrian should rise at five in the morning, then:

1. Run ½ mile at top speed up a hill.
2. Walk six miles at moderate pace.
3. Breakfast at about seven a.m. (beefsteaks, muttonchops, underdone with stale bread and old beer).
4. Walk six miles at moderate pace.
5. Lie in bed without clothes for ½ hour.
6. Walk four miles.
7. Dinner at four p.m. (beefsteaks, muttonchops with bread and beer as at breakfast).
8. Immediately after dinner, run ½ mile at top speed.
9. Walk six miles at moderate pace.
10. Bed at eight and repeat the next day.

Although one might question the virtue of sprinting a half mile with a stomach full of beefsteaks and old beer, it was an improvement over removing the spleen, a common procedure in the seventeenth and eighteenth centuries, born of the belief that it hindered speed.

The pedestrianism craze, and the popularity of Captain Barclay, led to the growth of running as a competitive sport. Most races were run for money, with financial backers each wagering on their champion. Events were held on fairgrounds and enclosed courses, and there was usually an admission fee. With improvement in the accuracy of watches and of measuring distances, it became possible to compete against the clock, setting records that others could try to beat.

Americans were soon swept up in the craze. In 1835, John Cox Stevens, a famous racehorse owner, promised $1,000 to anyone who could run ten miles in less than an hour. The contest attracted only nine competitors, but it drew a large crowd and much attention. A Connecticut farmer, Henry Stannard, managed to win the money with sixteen seconds to spare. Afterward, in an early prototype of the victory lap, he jumped on a horse and galloped around the course. The race inspired many imitators, including one that pitted Americans against Irishmen and Englishmen and drew 30,000 spectators.

Running soon became popular in schools and universities, and both Oxford and Cambridge fielded teams that competed against each other. These academic runners, however, were reluctant to compete with the "professionals," most of whom were working-class or lower-class. Out of this, the concept of the "amateur" runner was born: an athlete who would not compete for prize money and who did not make his living at the sport. This schism between professional and amateur runners would survive through the twentieth century, and it led athletes to take tortured measures to disguise their winnings, in order to earn a living.

By the late 1800s, there were races of all lengths on both sides of the Atlantic, including a six-day race for women held at Madison Square Garden. The women were required to wear heavy velvet dresses, and most sported boots or dance slippers on their feet. Bertha Von Berg, who walked and ran a total of 372 miles, won the inaugural event. The next year, Amy Howard won the race with a total of 409 miles, a record that stood for 102 years. For a time, six-day races were all the rage, and there were even several that pitted horses against men. In one famous event in Chicago, Michael Byrne beat the horse Speculator, who died in his stable on the last day of the race. Byrne went on to cover 578 miles, while his closest equine competitor ran only 563.

Out of this intense interest in running, the first Olympic Games were revived in 1896 by the Frenchman Baron de Coubertin, who conceived them as a means to encourage friendship and world peace. Until that time, most races were measured in British yards. But the French were on the metric system, and so the British 220 became the metric 200, the 440 became the 400, and the 880 became the 800. There was only the slightest difference in distance between 220 yards and 200 meters, so the translation worked fairly well. The mile, however, became the 1500 meters, making it about 120 yards shorter, and the 100-yard dash became the 100-meter dash, lengthening it by nearly 10 percent. The mile would survive as a separate race because of the interest in breaking the four-minute barrier, but the 100-yard dash would not.

The first marathon was set at a length of forty kilometers (about twenty-five miles) and intended to honor the ancient Greeks. The course ran from Marathon to Athens, along the approximate route taken by Pheidippides when he announced the Athenians' victory. There were twenty-five competitors, twenty-one of whom were Greek. The race was won by Spiridon Louis in a time of 2:58:50. For his efforts, he was promised "a new suit of clothes, free shaves and two cups of coffee per day for life, a dinner a day for a year and free laundry for life."

The first American marathon took place the following October. The route went from Stamford, Connecticut, to Columbus Circle in New York City, and the race was won by the New Yorker J. J. McDermott. On April 19, 1897, the first Boston Marathon was held with fifteen competitors. McDermott won this race as well, despite stopping five times (including to watch a Massachusetts Avenue funeral procession) and losing ten pounds over the course of the race.

Afterward, he vowed never to do it again, saying, "I hate to be called a quitter and a coward, but look at my feet."

In fact, he returned the following year and placed fourth.

On Tommy Leonard's fortieth birthday, Wednesday, August 15, 1973, the first "Falmouth marathon" was held at twelve noon. Ninety-three runners gathered outside the front door of the Captain Kidd in Woods Hole for a "7.3-mile race" to the Brothers Four in Falmouth Heights. An article in the *Falmouth Enterprise* promised a "mid-summer diversion" to "promote physical fitness." Along the course, it reported, "runners can expect girl volunteers to offer them paper cups filled with Gatoraid [*sic*], a lemonade drink containing glucose and salt, popular with runners of the [Boston] marathon." According to the paper, the other highlights included the following: "One lifeguard at Surf drive has offered to alert everybody on the beach when the runners approach. The Coast Guard will add to the finish line activities by firing some Very pistol flares from one of their small boats stationed close to shore." Some of the runners, the paper reported earnestly, "have taken the race seriously enough to give up cigarettes and beer until the finish line is crossed."

The town's new recreation department director, Rich Sherman, pitched in with posters and a race permit. Like John Carroll, Rich was a former middle-distance runner who had succumbed to Tommy's charisma. A race was just the thing for the dog days of August, the hot, sultry weeks when Labor Day's approach casts a pall over the joy that has been summer. Tommy promised a big turnout, with beer and hot dogs and an after-race party. Rich was in good shape, lean and square-jawed, and he decided to run the race himself. It would be a pleasant distraction from the bingo games, Ping-Pong tournaments, and other activities he usually managed.

A driving rain, however, put a damper on the promised festivities, although, given the noon start, it probably saved the runners from heat stroke. Tommy nearly missed the race when his car got stuck in three feet of water. Eventually, the stalwart few made it to the starting line, where John Carroll gave them prerace instructions. Then he stepped to the side under an umbrella and raised his starter's pistol. "Runners set!" he called.

He fired the gun, and the runners splashed off the line. They were wet and couldn't get any wetter, although at least it was warm. The few people in town who witnessed the spectacle thought they were crazy. But Woods Hole was used to oddballs: the town's July Fourth parade included graduate students dressed up as photosynthesis and mitosis. A few skinny guys and a handful of women, half-naked and soaked, made little impression. The runners went over the drawbridge, up the first hill past the post office, and around the corner by the library, and then they were gone.

Thirty-nine minutes and sixteen seconds later, Central Michigan University senior David Duba was the first to cross the finish line. He had heard about the race the night before while having drinks with some friends. As a result, he became a footnote in the history of the running boom. Tommy Leonard finished thirteenth. Rich Sherman, who never actually met John Carroll, his codirector, before the race, came in thirtieth, in 50:30.

The party followed at the Brothers Four. Awards were given: a blender, four shot glasses, a gift certificate to the Clam Shack. The rain let up, the stars came out, and twelve hours later the runners were still going strong. They danced the jitterbug and sang "I believe in music / I believe in love." It was the perfect ending to the perfect day, a birthday gift from the town of Falmouth to Tommy Leonard. There was only one thing that would have made him happier. But the Olympic champion was busy buying books and registering for classes. Frank Shorter's last year of law school was more important than a road race in the middle of the week in an obscure town on Cape Cod, Massachusetts.

Bill Rodgers cruises to an easy victory over Marty Liquori
in the 1974 Falmouth Road Race.

Courtesy Falmouth Historical Society

4

"Will Rogers" and the Car
He Drove In With (1974)

*Every race you do, every step you take is a journey,
and once you get going, nothing can stop you.*

— BILL RODGERS

THE MEMBERS OF THE Greater Boston Track Club assembled at the Eliot Lounge after their Tuesday and Thursday night track workouts at Boston College. Tommy Leonard poured, the beer flowed, and Coach Bill Squires held forth. This race, and that one; this champion, and that one. They were small fish in a small pond, but that didn't stop the talkers.

Bill Rodgers listened, but he didn't say much. He had just returned from a disastrous trip to California, which had followed his disastrous first attempt at the Boston Marathon. Unaccustomed to the distance, and in warm conditions, he'd dropped out of the race after twenty miles. He blamed the heat for his poor performance, so he decided to move to California with his girlfriend, Ellen Lalone, to train in a warmer climate. They drove across the country in a van, slept at rest stops, and arrived in Pasadena. But the move quickly proved to be a mistake. They had no money and no place to live, and Rodgers hated the cars, the people, and even the weather. They stayed only two days, then turned around and drove all the way back to Boston.

For six months, they lived on food stamps until Rodgers finally got a job working with developmentally disabled adults. He had been running with the Boston Athletic Association, whose coach, Jock Semple, was infamous for attempting to yank Kathrine Switzer out of the all-male Boston Marathon in 1967. (Her boyfriend decked him, and she finished the race.) But Rodgers found himself going for long runs with friends on the GBTC and soon gravitated toward the team. In late 1973, however, he hadn't officially joined the club, so he sat in the Eliot nursing his beer and let the others do the talking.

Sitting still did not come easily to Rodgers. As a boy, he spent hours in a big green field chasing down tiger swallowtail, red admiral, and red-spotted purple butterflies. He loved running through open fields and the feel of grass between his bare toes. He was skinny, with blue eyes and blond hair that always fell in front of his face. When he wasn't running, he was playing football, hunting squirrels and ducks with a BB gun, stealing balls from the nearby golf course or corn from a local farmer's field, or hiking in the woods with friends. In school, it was hard for him to concentrate, and he often spent his time daydreaming and staring out the window, waiting for the day to end so that he could get outside and move.

It was as a sophomore in high school that he discovered he was the fastest kid in the mile in his gym class. After that, he joined the cross-country and track teams, eventually running a 4:28 mile and a 2:07 half-mile, the kind of times that get a kid noticed locally and ignored nationally. In truth, he was lazy. He looked for any excuse not to train: cold, rain, a haircut. At best, he would run two to three miles a day, spending most of his time doing shorter intervals on the track. Even then, people thought he was a little nutty, running around the neighborhood. In 1963, no one jogged, and except for the Olympics, running was only something one did to catch a train or escape the cops. Rodgers was happy enough to run, but he hated racing, and he didn't like competing at all. He would have preferred, like Ferdinand the bull, to entertain himself amid the flowers all day long.

When he went away to college, at Wesleyan University in Middletown, Connecticut, he had no great plans to continue his running. Wesleyan was a small school, with only 1,400 undergraduates and 250 graduate students at that time. But with an average SAT score in the 95th percentile, it was also one of the most competitive schools in the country. Along with Williams and Amherst Colleges, Wesleyan was part of the Little Three, schools known for their academic excellence, not their sports prowess. As members of NCAA Division III, they were prohibited from granting athletic scholarships, and their recruiting pitch focused more on class size than gym size. No one harbored any illusions that Little Three students would go on to be anything but doctors, lawyers, and bankers. The number of graduates who had professional sports careers could be counted on two hands.

In 1968, however, a Wesleyan senior named Amby Burfoot won the Boston Marathon. It was a remarkable victory, made all the more impressive by the fact that Burfoot essentially trained himself. Wesleyan's track coach was a former Detroit Tigers first baseman who kept a spittoon in his office. Yet Burfoot ran twice a day, logging more than one hundred miles a week. What he knew about running he'd learned from his high school coach in Groton, Connecticut, a former Boston Marathon winner himself. Under his tutelage, Amby became a standout at Fitch Senior High School, and in his senior year he won the state two-mile championship.

Rodgers had competed against Burfoot's younger brother in Connecticut races and usually beat him. Thus he was persona non grata around the Burfoot household. It didn't help his standing when, upon his arrival at college, Rodgers broke Wesleyan's cross-country course record. The next week, Burfoot went out and promptly broke it again. He was not about to let a freshman take his crown. Running, however, was thicker than blood. Soon the two men became inseparable friends, and Burfoot's influence on

Rodgers would later become a crucial part of the story Rodgers told about himself.

Burfoot was as focused and organized as Rodgers was flaky and disorganized. In addition to double workouts, Burfoot ran twenty-five miles every Sunday morning. Rodgers stayed in bed, often sleeping off a beer-and-cigarette buzz, but he would drag himself outside and join Amby as he crossed the campus for his last ten miles. Once, he even completed the entire twenty-five. He knew he lacked Amby's dedication, and he believed he lacked Amby's talent, but he found the runs refreshing and always felt better for them.

When Burfoot won the Boston Marathon in 1968, it had little immediate effect on Rodgers. Indeed, there was no television coverage and only a few newspaper articles about the event. It was a long haul in a cold city, and despite its pedigree, the marathon was still an event for aficionados. The race was not something Rodgers dreamed about running, let alone running well, but his friend's victory lodged in the back of his mind. He still viewed Burfoot as out of his league, but the idea that someone with whom he trained could win Boston planted a seed that would sprout a champion.

Rodgers had talent, but he ran on fumes. He trained with Amby and competed with the team, but he didn't push any harder than necessary. He was not a striver or a planner. Despite the fact that both his parents were teachers, he had no larger ambitions than to hang out, run when he could, smoke cigarettes, and sleep late. He was as lackadaisical about his schoolwork as he was about his running, and he had no desire to follow the corporate path of so many of his Wesleyan classmates. As he saw it, "too many people were too carried away with the intellectual side of life in general." Intelligence was a complicated thing, he believed, and meant more than good grades and graduate degrees.

The one thing he knew for certain was that he wasn't going to serve in the Vietnam War. His objection to fighting (and possibly dying) for a cause in which he did not believe consumed him. It made everything else, including his running, seem trivial. For a while, he nurtured dreams of fleeing the country, working on a freighter in New Zealand, leaving his friends and family behind forever. The war had polarized the nation, and young men like him bore its brunt. Conscription was not voluntary; military service not an abstraction. More than 50,000 U.S. soldiers died in Southeast Asia (along with millions of Vietnamese and Cambodians), and on college campuses, the resistance to U.S. involvement had reached a fever pitch, culminating in the killing of four students at Kent State University by the National Guard. At liberal Wesleyan, students wore black armbands and took to the quad to mourn them.

In his senior year, without Amby to push him, Rodgers's motivation flagged. By January, he had stopped running completely. What was the point, really? In a few months, the real world would come knocking, and running would become a thing of the past, tossed into the basement along with his butterfly nets and old rubber boots. Instead, all his energy went into applying for conscientious objector status, his only safe means to stay in the country without an educational deferment or a medical exemption. Without it, he feared, he really would have to flee.

In the spring, to his great relief, his CO status was granted. As an alternative to serving overseas, he was permitted to do community service at home. A friend helped him get a job at Peter Bent Brigham Hospital in Boston, and for a time it seemed as if he had dodged a bullet.

The job, however, was the lowest of the low, and he quickly came to hate it. His responsibilities included transporting blood samples to the lab, moving sick patients around the hospital, and wheeling dead bodies to the morgue. He was paid the paltry sum of $75 a week and treated poorly by the doctors — in his view because he did not want to go to Vietnam. He did not object to menial labor, but he despised the menial treatment by the high and mighty. In short, as he later noted, he was "down, aimless, unmotivated, and without direction."

His one indulgence was a motorcycle he bought with nearly all his money: $1,000. On it, he wandered for a year — both literally and metaphorically — driving around Boston, smoking and drinking, growing his hair long, and hanging out with his older brother, Charlie, their childhood friend Jason Kehoe, and his girlfriend, Ellen Lalone, whom he had met at a bar in Cambridge.

In April 1971, he was living near Symphony Hall, along the Boston Marathon route. He had never actually seen the race, and for the first time he was struck by the huge crowd and the carnival atmosphere. He watched several former college teammates and rivals finish among the elite. It was thrilling but also sobering. At this point, he was up to two packs of cigarettes a day and about as far away from attempting a marathon as a hedgehog.

Then two things happened that changed his life. First, his motorcycle was stolen. With no means of transportation, Rodgers began to jog the mile and a half to work. Then he was fired from his job for trying to organize the nonunion employees.

Unemployed, out of shape, and with winter approaching, Rodgers still owed the government another six months of service. But as a conscientious objector fired for cause, he was essentially unemployable. No decent employer would touch him. Instead, he survived on handouts and Ellen's meager earnings, which was humiliating and emasculating. Rodgers knew he needed something to ward off depression and to give his days order. He went back to running, he said, because "it was all I knew, all I had left."

With no money, he ran in blue jeans and tattered T-shirts. His eating habits had always been eccentric — ketchup on brownies, mayonnaise on pizza, peanut butter and bacon bits — so stuffing his face with dinner rolls at the diner was not unusual for him. He joined the local YMCA and ran on its tiny indoor track, twelve laps to the mile. The track was slanted and uneven, but he didn't mind. He lost himself in the monotony, running 120 laps in a session, sweating out the poisons of nicotine and despair.

Soon he graduated to loops around Jamaica Pond in the Jamaica Plain section of Boston. Each loop was about 1.6 miles, and he ran around and around, as many as fourteen times. That a runner in a town like Boston, with its routes along the Charles River and Newton Hills, would choose instead to circle a small urban pond was a symptom of what Rodgers later came to recognize as ADHD. Although he was often described as spacy and disorganized — the race director of the Boston Marathon once said Rodgers was lucky the course had only five turns — a common symptom of ADHD is hyperfocus. People with the disorder are often unable to transition from one task they find pleasurable to a different task and can spend hours completely immersed in their present activity. Among athletes, this type of hyperfocus is often called being in the zone.

ADHD also explained Rodgers's preference for long, monotonous runs and his aversion to speed work. Running shorter intervals on the track requires constant starting and stopping, regular pacing, and a stopwatch — all the things that someone who hates transitions and has problems with organization will resist. Thus, unlike Frank Shorter or Alberto Salazar, Rodgers was never ranked among the top ten in the 5000 meters or 10,000 meters, and his fastest time for one mile was just a handful of seconds quicker than his average pace for twenty-six.

But on the roads, Rodgers was unstoppable. Less than a year after his return to running, he finished third in a twenty-mile race won by Amby Burfoot. A month later, he finished second in the New England AAU thirty-kilometer championships, and a few weeks after that, he won a twelve-mile race in under sixty minutes — a pace faster than five minutes per mile. Seeing him on the roads, someone might think a strong wind could blow him off course. Mop-topped and floppy-gaited, he was only five foot nine and about 130 pounds. When he ran, he was slightly pigeon-toed, and his head bobbed like a chicken's. But his leg turnover was quick, and his size was actually ideal for the longer distances.

Rodgers may have goofed off in college, but he hated being unemployed. It put a great strain on his relationship with Ellen and left him feeling impotent and enraged. His experiences at the hospital had radicalized him, and he was furious at the government for forcing him into penury. He managed to get a job at Arby's but quit after only one night, feeling demeaned by the silly uniforms and the extremely low pay. He would rather have his dignity and his running than a stupid hat and a cheeseburger.

He set his sights on the 1973 Boston Marathon. Frank Shorter had electrified the running community by winning the marathon at the Munich Olympics. Rodgers did not consider himself in the same league as Shorter, yet the marathon felt like something he could do — something he *had* to do. He saw the race as one very long run, something that Amby had managed in college, and he practiced for it that way. His training runs were all done at seven minutes per mile, and he did no speed work. He figured that he had run the twelve-mile race at a sub-five-minute pace, so all he had to do was maintain that speed for another fourteen miles. The marathon gave him a specific goal, and it also became a way to redeem a sad and frustrating period in his life, a time when nothing seemed to be right and everything around him had fallen to pieces. Running was a means to control the madness and chaos of a world in flux, and it became his salvation.

But the race was a disaster. Rodgers never ran well in the heat, and his lack of speed work left him unprepared for the surges the leaders threw at him in the midst of running twenty-six miles. He dropped out at twenty miles just as he hit the "wall" — the point at which his body had burned through all its stored glycogen — and went home bitter and ashamed. His failure was made worse by the importance he had attached to the race, so that dropping out felt like something larger and more profound than it actually was. It clung to him like a bad smell and ultimately motivated his impulsive and foolhardy move to California.

By the time he returned, he had stopped running. It was June, and the weather turned warm and lovely. In Boston, the trees blossomed along the Charles, and the sky sparkled. Like a newborn, Rodgers took a few steps outdoors and found that his legs still worked. Boston's running community was small and tight-knit, and although members of the BAA and the GBTC competed against one another, it was a friendly rivalry with plenty of crossbreeding. Even after Rodgers jumped ship for the GBTC, he still joined friends from the BAA on the roads.

When winter arrived, he felt that his training was getting back to its pre-California level. In November, he finished and won his first marathon in Lowell, Massachusetts, with a time of 2:28. During the race, he deliberately held back and focused more on finishing than on setting any record. But completing the race gave his confidence a boost and convinced him that the distance was not insurmountable. On January 8, 1974, he was second in a two-mile indoor race at Northeastern University (running 9:08.5). On January 9, he ran twenty miles in nine inches of snow around Jamaica Pond. The next day, he ran another twenty in three more inches. His legs were "achey and sore," he wrote in his training log, but "fortunately it was light and dry powdery snow."

Now there was nothing between him and the Boston Marathon. With his GBTC teammates, he trained on Heartbreak Hill (actually a series of four hills between miles 16 and 20). He joined the team on the track and forced himself to do speed workouts. He familiarized himself with the marathon course so that he knew every dip and climb, every blind curve and open straightaway. He ran in the morning and at night, and when he wasn't running, he dreamed about it.

On April 15, he completed his first Boston Marathon. His time was 2:19:34, good enough for fourteenth place. More important, he was in fourth after twenty miles but fell back over the final six. For the first time, he had run with the best and held his own. It convinced him that with a little better training, a little more effort, and some favorable weather conditions, he could be a contender. That chance would come sooner than he expected, in a place he didn't anticipate.

• • •

Bill Rodgers was a haphazard runner. The guiding principle in his training was mileage. What he knew about speed, he learned on the fly and then tried to forget. It was Coach Squires who introduced him to serious interval training, and that would make all the difference. Although he never enjoyed the rigid routine, working with a team helped him to concentrate and to overcome his natural aversion to the stopwatch.

The great Finnish distance runner Paavo Nurmi was one of the first practitioners of the art of speed. He built his training around "terraces," alternating hard effort and rest, and he trained twice a day. In the 1924 Olympics, fifty-six minutes after he won the 1500 meters, he won the 5000. He also won the 10,000-meter cross-country race and the 3000-meter team race. His routine was emulated by the Swedes, who developed the *fartlek* (speed play) method, which consisted of varying bursts of speed during a continuous run of longer distances.

But the real breakthrough in modern training came from Woldemar Gerschler, a physical education professor at Turenne College in Germany. In the 1930s, working with cardiologist Herbert Reindel, he discovered that by forcing the heart to beat intensely for short periods and then recover, a runner could enlarge his heart muscle and increase his endurance. This so-called interval method called for running hard enough to increase the heart rate to about 180 beats per minute, then permitting 90 seconds of recovery, during which the heart rate should go down to 120 beats or lower. If it did not, the workout was over. After twenty-one days of interval training, Gerschler showed, heart volume could be increased by 20 percent.

Emil Zátopek, from Czechoslovakia, was probably the most famous proponent of interval training. His routine consisted of multiple 200- and 400-meter repeats, usually thirty at a time. At one point, he ran sixty 400-meter repeats each day for ten days. Like Nurmi, his training theory was simple: run as hard as possible as much as possible. He was famous for his lurching, head-rolling form, so ugly that one commentator noted, "Zatopek ran like a man who had been stabbed through the heart." But he was fast. In the 1948 Olympics, he won the gold medal in the 10,000 meters and the silver in the 5000 (losing by one meter). Between 1948 and 1952, he won every single 5000- and 10,000-meter race he entered. In the 1952 Olympics, he not only won gold at both 5000 and 10,000 meters, but he also decided at the last minute to run the marathon (his first ever). He won that event as well, setting a new Olympic record. To this day, he remains the only runner to have won a gold medal on the track and in the marathon at the Olympics.

The efforts and accomplishments of Nurmi, Zátopek, and the Swedish runners Gunder Hägg and Arne Andersson played a crucial role in the assault on the four-minute-mile "barrier." By 1945, in a series of races over a four-year period, Hägg and Andersson had lowered the record from 4:06.2 to 4:01.4. Within the year, however, both men were declared "professionals" for accepting too much expense money, and it would be nearly another decade before the charge would continue. It arose, in large part, out of Roger Bannister's failure to win the 1500 meters at the 1952 Olympics.

Bannister was the top-ranked miler in the world in 1951 (with a personal best of 4:07.8), but at the Olympics an extra heat was added in the 1500 meters, requiring him to run three races in three consecutive days. Because he was in medical school, he'd had little time to train, and the extra race took its toll on his legs. He finished fourth and went home without a medal. Looking for a way to distinguish himself and avenge his loss, and knowing that his medical career would prevent him from racing through the next Olympics, he set a goal to be the first man to go under four minutes in the mile.

With only about thirty minutes to run between his classes, Bannister's interval training consisted of ten 440-yard laps on the track with a two-minute recovery between laps. If he could run each at 60 seconds per lap, he believed, he could break four minutes. At first, he was averaging 63 seconds. By April 1954, he had brought that down to 61 seconds. Frustrated by his inability to go faster, he went on a four-day rock-climbing trip with his training partner, Chris Brasher. When he returned, he discovered that he was able to run his laps at 59 seconds. He knew then that he was ready for his attempt at the record.

On May 6, 1954, at the Iffley Road Track in Oxford, England, Bannister was joined by Brasher and Chris Chataway. The plan was for Brasher to take the lead through the half-mile mark, then have Chataway lead through the three-quarter-mile mark. After that, Bannister was on his own. At first, it seemed as if the wind might be too strong for anyone to achieve a good time, and it was raining as well, but about an hour before the race, the wind calmed down and the rain stopped. The mile was part of a track meet between the British Amateur Athletic Association and Oxford University, and it included three other runners besides Bannister, Chataway, and Brasher. (For the record, the AAA won, 64–34.) Few of the three thousand spectators knew what the three men planned to do.

Brasher did his job for the first lap, pulling them through at 57.5. Bannister (incorrectly) thought the pace was too slow, and he shouted for Brasher to pick it up. At the half-mile mark, the runners went through at 1:58. Chataway then took over, pacing Bannister through the three-quarter-mile mark at 3:00.5. About three hundred yards from the finish, Chataway slowed down (the result, no doubt, of smoking "only" seven cigarettes per day during racing season), and Bannister was alone. He started sprinting, knowing that he had to run faster than 59.5 seconds for the last lap. With the crowd cheering, now realizing something special was occurring, he crossed the line and fell into the arms of his friend, the Reverend Nicholas Stacey.

The race was narrated for BBC Radio by Harold Abrahams (of *Chariots of Fire* fame), and as fans mobbed Bannister, the track announcement was made by Norris McWhirter (who later published and edited the *Guinness Book of World Records*). McWhirter drew out the announcement for the maximum possible suspense:

60

Ladies and gentlemen, here is the result of event 9, the one mile: 1st, No. 41, R. G. Bannister, Amateur Athletic Association and formerly of Exeter and Merton Colleges, Oxford, with a time which is a new meeting and track record, and which — subject to ratification — will be a new English Native, British National, All-Comers, European, British Empire and World Record. The time was 3 minutes . . .

The rest was lost in the roar of the crowd. Bannister had run 3:59.4 and become the first man to run under four minutes for the mile.

The quest to break the four-minute mile probably had as profound an effect on the sport of running throughout the world as Shorter's victory at Munich would have in the United States eighteen years later. It set in motion a public fascination with the sport and affirmed for distance runners the importance of speed in addition to stamina. If it worked for Bannister, Zátopek, and Nurmi, the same principles should apply to Shorter, Rodgers, and Salazar. The world was about to witness the revolution.

August 18, 1974, was hot and humid. By 10 a.m., the sun was a sticky yellow ball and the sky a gauzy blue. Falmouth Road Race organizers had predicted two hundred runners; at race time, there were more than four hundred. Volunteers struggled to sign them up in time for the start, and the recreation center was a scene of confusion and chaos. Rich Sherman scrambled to print out enough applications before leaving for the race himself. No one complained, however. It was summer, everyone was in shorts and tank tops, and a feeling of adventure was in the air. For two bucks, they got to participate in a moving street party. When they finished, there would be cold beer and soda, hot dogs, and watermelon waiting for them. John Carroll promised that prizes would be given in several categories. "So don't give up just because we have some great runners lined up," he told them.

Tommy Leonard had convinced the Town of Falmouth to move the race to a Sunday, even though it would conflict with beach traffic. He wrote a letter to Frank Shorter, pleading his case, but Shorter's father politely declined the invitation on his son's behalf. (Shorter was racing in Warsaw, Poland.) Although Tommy failed to get the celebrity runner he wanted, he scored a coup by securing a commitment from Marty Liquori, ranked number one in the mile in 1971 and, along with Jim Ryun, the fastest miler in the United States at the time. Liquori's brother, Steve, was a regular at the Eliot Lounge, and Tommy plied him with beers until he agreed to convince Marty to run. Tommy promised there would be "bikini-clad girls" handing out drinks; a bathtub full of clam chowder for the finishers, courtesy of the Captain Kidd; and a band playing "When Irish Eyes Are Smiling" at the finish line. If the race didn't get five hundred runners, he promised to "do a swan dive off the Bourne Bridge."

Liquori came in from New Jersey for the race. He had spent six weeks racing in Europe, where he ran a 3:56.2 mile in Sweden. Although he was the only U.S. runner to defeat the legendary Ryun, and only the third high schooler to run a sub-four-minute mile, Liquori went on to become one of the United States' best 5000-meter runners. In fact, a few months before Falmouth, he had placed fifth in the AAU national championships and planned to compete in the event at the 1976 Olympics. Despite press reports after the race that made it seem as if Falmouth was longer than his reach, he was clearly prepared to run the distance and was the overwhelming favorite.

The GBTC came out in force. Three of the club's athletes would finish in the top five, eight in the top twenty. Bill Rodgers drove down with Ellen Lalone. Like his teammates, he had been talked into racing by Tommy. At the time, it took very little to get some of the best athletes in the United States to travel two hours or more to run a race. For Rodgers, it was the bikini-clad girls. For Liquori, it was the free hotel room on the Cape. For many others, it was simply the opportunity to check out a new course, compete with friends, have an adventure. Road racing would never pay their bills, and even a major win at Boston or New York came with little more than a commemorative plate. Amateur rules prevented them from taking money, and there was no money available in any event. To provide prizes for the winners at Falmouth, Tommy went door-to-door on Main Street, to the hardware store, the bakery, the restaurants, and the dry cleaner.

The runners came dressed for the heat and humidity. As the local newspaper noted, most were wearing "head bands, tee shirts, loose flared legged shorts and the expensive, low cut soft padded running shoes now worn by all of those who take it seriously, as most of those running obviously did." Nevertheless, when it was over, six people were taken to the hospital, and two young men were admitted to the ICU.

As for the race itself, it was no contest. Rodgers had a slight lead at the first mile, one hundred yards by the second mile, and three hundred yards when they hit Surf Drive. After that, he continued to pull away, running easily and well within himself, and winning by more than a minute. "Zapped M. Liquori! O What glory!" he wrote in his running log. His time of 34:16 broke the course record by five minutes.

For his efforts, he won a toaster, two tickets for the ferry to Martha's Vineyard, and a dinner for two at the Medieval Manor in Boston. He was such an unknown that in the official race results, he was listed as "Will Rogers." The next day, Joe Concannon compounded the error in a *Boston Globe* article headlined "Rogers Catches Miler Liquori Out of Natural Element." Two paragraphs of the article were devoted to "Will Rogers" and the remaining nine to Liquori. But Rodgers was a good sport; he joined well-wishers and fellow runners at the Brothers Four for beers and live music. He didn't even mind when, as a parting gift, his car was towed by the Falmouth police.

Alberto Salazar after receiving intravenous fluids
at the Falmouth Road Race.

Courtesy Charlie Rodgers

5

Cuba Libre (1965–1975)

I never considered myself fast. I was just able to endure.

— ALBERTO SALAZAR

THE SIXTEEN-YEAR-OLD BOY on the track was painfully thin: six feet tall, but only 130 pounds after a good meal. His dark eyes scowled at the competition. It was July 4, 1975, and on the Nebraska track the temperature was close to 122 degrees. Alberto Salazar had qualified for this race by finishing second to North Carolina State standout Ralph King one month earlier at the junior outdoor championships in Knoxville, Tennessee. Now he faced King again, as well as the USSR junior national team, in the 5000 meters. He had already made a name for himself in New England, setting every distance record at Wayland High School and breaking the Massachusetts two-mile scholastic record. But he had never run against international competition before and never run in a venue as hot as Nebraska in July.

The other runners didn't know what to expect of him. He certainly didn't look intimidating, despite his glowering eyes and vaguely Middle Eastern look. Even King, who had beaten him several weeks earlier, thought the kid had a lot of talent but it would be several more years before he was truly a threat. Salazar, however, didn't care what the others thought; he never did. He was not a subtle runner — he didn't feint or dodge and weave — and he wasn't a pretty one. He ran hard and fast from the start and made his competition think about what he was thinking instead.

Growing up in New England, Alberto had learned to ignore the taunts of his white-bread classmates, who found the Salazar family strange and different. His father had been close friends with Fidel Castro and had fought beside him and Che Guevara in the Cuban Revolution. But José Salazar watched with growing dismay as the revolution turned from democracy into autocracy and Castro turned Cuba into a godless Marxist state. He fled Cuba for Miami in October 1960 and spent the next six months training for the Bay of Pigs invasion. But when the invasion was crushed by Castro's forces, he was left a stranger in a strange land, *el exilio,* scheming and plotting a triumphant return to his homeland. He gave up on Florida, but not his dreams, and moved his newly immigrated family north to Wayland, Massachusetts, in 1968.

His son Alberto was raised in the shadow of his obsession. Across the family table, there were always angry men yelling in Spanish. Cigarettes and coffee stains darkened their fingers. Once, one of the men left the house and returned with a machine gun. Impassioned, embattled, impotent, and crazed, the Cuban exile community's imprint on Alberto and his brothers and sisters was profound. He grew up both embarrassed and proud of his father's devotion, shy and fierce, avoiding attention yet standing out. He wanted a normal American kid's life — hot dogs and macaroni and cheese — yet he wanted to prove himself, to make his father proud.

But the Salazar home would never resemble the houses with the white picket fences of its neighbors. To make matters worse, Alberto was skinny, gangly, and awkward, a far cry from the blond-haired, blue-eyed football captain. At school, they called him "Castro Convertible." His oldest brother, Ricardo, shared Alberto's dark eyes and olive skin, but he was a natural athlete, a miler who won a scholarship to the U.S. Naval Academy in Annapolis. As the third son, four years younger than Ricardo and two years younger than José Jr., Alberto always had to work a little harder to get his father's attention. And in high school, even when he started breaking records, he never quite fit in among the privileged sons and daughters of the Yankee bankers and lawyers.

Years later, friends would say that Salazar's success was the result of his constant desire to please a domineering father and outshine a golden older brother. His college roommate and teammate, Rudy Chapa, whose family was Mexican, said they both shared an immigrant's mentality: a chip on the shoulder and a need to prove their worth. His older GBTC teammate Kirk Pfrangle claimed that Salazar's tenacity was a reaction to his authoritarian father, a man who saw the world in black and white, church and state, Catholic deities and godless Communists. Salazar himself said he grew up with a rage he couldn't explain, a father who screamed at him during training runs, "A Salazar never quits!"

In his memoir, *14 Minutes,* he tells the story of the time some boys broke a light bulb at his younger brother's birthday party. His father "freaked out" and blamed nine-year-old Alberto because his mother had left him "in charge" of organizing the games. His father insisted on fixing the light immediately and left the party to go to the store for a replacement. While he was gone, police cars whipped by the house on their way to Salters Pond, where some boys had been sailing on a raft. One of the boys had hit his head and drowned.

The party broke up in the excitement, and Alberto ran down to the pond to watch as police divers found the boy and tried, unsuccessfully, to resuscitate him. It was a traumatic scene — the flashing blue lights, the boy's deathly white skin, the unfathomable blackness of the water — and after his initial fascination, Alberto ran home to his mother, crying. When his father returned, he blamed his son for the boy's death: if Alberto had not allowed his brother's friends to break the light, his father would not have had to run out for a replacement and could have saved the drowned boy.

Salazar forgave his father's "twisted logic," the result, he wrote, of the "shock at the terrible accident, combined with his embarrassment at overreacting to the busted lamp and guilt about leaving the house." But like any gifted child, Alberto learned that making his father happy was the only way to avoid his anger. And nothing made his father happier than Alberto's running. So he ran, and yet the happiness he sought eluded him.

Temperament, however, is also hard-wired, and Salazar was no exception. As a boy, he'd go into a "black funk" after a bad race, questioning his very existence and not being able to eat or sleep for days. In midlife, he suffered bouts of depression that required medication to keep him from spiraling down into despair. His moods swung from anger to despondence. He became notorious for his refusal to speak with the press, for holding back a part of himself, for not suffering fools (or anyone) gladly. Running was a form of self-medication that kept his demons at bay by pumping neurotransmitters into his system. He craved the rush running gave him, and as the years passed he needed to run farther, longer, and harder to get the same thrill.

Running is also an evolutionary imperative. Human beings may not be the fastest animals on the planet (in fact, we are slower than warthogs, grizzly bears, and the ordinary housecat), but we are one of the few animals built to run long distances. Our feet are rigid, with an arch for propulsion and shock absorption. The tendons in our legs store energy and release it efficiently. Our thin waists and relatively large butt muscles help keep us upright and stable. More important, our hairlessness, two million sweat glands, and ability to breathe through our mouths enabled our forebears to stay cool as they hunted prey over long distances, literally running it to the ground.

The development of the human brain was a direct result of this "endurance hunting." Because tracking prey over long distances requires smarts, natural selection favored intelligence over brute strength. Endurance hunting also requires perseverance and the ability to withstand great pain to envision the end result. According to zoologist Bernd Heinrich, "We see our 'prey' before us even if it has disappeared behind hills or in the mist. And it is this vision that becomes our key motivator at these moments. It is the power of visualization that enables us to reach out toward the future, whether our goal is to bring down a mammoth, write a book, or set a new record time in a race."

Salazar had visualization in spades. It was his brother Ricardo who set him on the path. Stopwatch in hand, Ricardo would time the neighborhood kids in the fifty-yard dash or in races around the house. Alberto was not the fastest, but he could keep going when the other kids became breathless. In games of tag, he would always win because his pursuers grew tired of chasing him. When he wasn't running with Ricardo, he would run around the block and through the open fields near his house. In sixth grade, he won the Bowers Elementary School 600-yard race. In eighth grade, he ran two junior varsity cross-country races and won them both. It was then, he wrote, that "I knew I wanted to be a champion runner, the best in the world, an Olympic gold medalist."

When he ran, he was not the skinny Castro Convertible, but an American champion. Ricardo, who at that point was one of the top cross-country runners in high school, pushed him to train harder and run faster. In Alberto's freshman year, he entered a twenty-mile road race near his home. No coach would ever have recommended it, but for Alberto it was a way to prove his mettle not just to Ricardo but to his father as well. Although he had to walk partway, he finished the race, and discovered there was pleasure in pushing through great pain. He may not have shared his brother's fast-twitch muscle fibers, but he had the constitution of a martyr or a saint.

In his sophomore year, he won the state Class C cross-country title. By his junior year, he held the national record for his age group in the two-mile. Everyone in the running community knew his name, and he was touted by *Track & Field News* as the "young distance phenom . . . with a one way flight to stardom."

He came to the attention of a decent sub-elite runner named Kirk Pfrangle, the kind of guy who goes to high school track meets for fun. Although Salazar ran like a duck (butt down, feet splayed), in a two-mile indoor track race he simply blew away the rest of the field. Salazar clearly outclassed his Wayland teammates, and his coach was in over his head. For Pfrangle, it was like watching a Little League game and suddenly having Derek Jeter show up to play shortstop. Not only was it unfair to the other players, but it changed the dynamics of the game.

At the time, Pfrangle was training with a new running club in Boston. He approached Salazar and asked if the boy wanted to run with them. Salazar shrugged and said he would have to check with his father. The elder Salazar regarded Pfrangle with suspicion. Who was this guy stepping out of the stands and offering to drive his son into Boston? Pfrangle could be anything: a pederast, a double agent, an assassin. Years later, when Alberto went to compete in the Soviet Union, his father was convinced he would be kidnapped by Cuban agents and held hostage. It was the exile's paranoia, fear writ large. But Alberto prevailed upon his father to let him run with the club, and soon Pfrangle was driving him to Tufts and Boston College for regular workouts with the GBTC.

Like the Florida Track Club, the GBTC was one of the few options for runners without a collegiate affiliation to train and race. In those early years, a running club was about as common as sushi, and just as strange. Coach Squires had a day job at Boston College and coached the team for free. Squires was something of a legend in track circles: part guru, part flake. Listening to him was like trying to catch a fish barehanded: just when you thought you had it, it wriggled away. When the team would drive to New York City to run in the Millrose Games, he'd be sitting in the back seat giving advice. After the races, he'd still be talking over beers at the Blarney Stone.

Then on the long ride home, he'd continue the conversation with the driver as everyone else fell asleep. This suited his charges just fine. Squires filled the empty spaces that otherwise would have been occupied by nerves and anticipation.

He had his theories about running, although they were not always clearly expressed. What his runners remember most about him is his total faith in their ability and his credo of commitment, perseverance, and hill work. The specific workouts they did under his command were not nearly as important as the bonds that held the club together. Squires was the Joe Torre of his era: blessed with a team of incredibly talented athletes who probably would have succeeded under anyone's tutelage, and knowledgeable enough about the sport not to hurt them.

They called Salazar "the Rookie," which wasn't the most inventive nickname, but it reminded them to watch their language in his presence. When he first showed up with Pfrangle on a Tuesday night, Squires wasn't impressed. Salazar was skinny and looked malnourished, and there was that ugly running gait. Squires put him in the B group to see if he could hold on. He did more than that. He quickly outpaced everyone in the group. The next week he was running with the best runners on the team, grinding out thousand-yard repeats. The pace exhausted him, but he would not quit. He never backed off, and he never dropped out. "The one thing a long-distance runner cannot afford to do," he wrote later, "is let up."

This was a sixteen-year-old kid training with runners a decade older, but it didn't faze him. Some of his teammates remember him as "standoffish" or "unfriendly." Others excused his attitude as the natural aversion of a sixteen-year-old to men a decade older. Even at that age, however, Salazar believed he was better than all his GBTC teammates — men who would become champions in their own right. All, that is, except Bill Rodgers.

Outside the New England running community, Rodgers was still an unknown. But he was racking up victories on the roads and clearly was the best distance runner on the team. Salazar keyed off the older man's workouts and kept him close when they ran the Newton Hills, with Squires on a bicycle counting off intervals. Rodgers was the one to watch, the one to beat, and Salazar tucked in behind his shoulder and ran in his draft.

In June, Coach Squires entered him in the 5000 meters at the junior outdoor track-and field championships in Knoxville. Although he finished second to Ralph King, who was three years older, his time equaled the world record for a sixteen-year-old, set previously by Craig Virgin. Suddenly, he was no longer just a top Massachusetts or even a top U.S. runner; he was a world record holder, in heady company with Virgin, the NCAA and Big Ten cross-country champion. He was now certifiably faster than most of his GBTC teammates, although that didn't stop them from continuing to refer to him as "the Rookie."

A few weeks later, as a result of that race, he was on the track in Nebraska, taking on King and the USSR junior national team. Alberto's father despised the Soviet Union almost as much as Cuba. Not only was it an evil, godless empire, but its support for Castro propped up that regime when it rightly should have fallen. When Alberto won the race, José saw it as a validation of all that was good and moral, as well as confirming the Salazars' place in toppling tyranny wherever it might be found.

As for Alberto, he ended up in the medical tent with an IV in his arm. It was the first time he faced down death, but it would not be the last. Maybe his father was right: God really did smile on the Salazars.

Steve Prefontaine and Frank Shorter on the track in Oregon.

6

The Good Die Young (May 30, 1975)

I've always had a survivor's guilt . . .
If only I had talked to him for thirty seconds more.
— FRANK SHORTER

ALMOUTH WAS THE FURTHEST thing from Frank Shorter's mind when he returned to Gainesville after Munich. He was a gold medalist, but he was no Mark Spitz. The president didn't call, and no one offered him the cover of a Wheaties box. Beneath the surface, a boom was brewing, but as Shorter saw it, "I might as well have won my gold medal in archery, cycling, or Greco-Roman wrestling."

Instead, Louis Mills, the chief executive of Orange County, New York, invited him to a testimonial dinner in his honor in his hometown of Middletown. More than two hundred people attended, and Shorter was presented with the key to the city (i.e., the downtown strip). His friends and former neighbors had no idea what the marathon was, but the local boy had done good, and that was enough for them.

Shorter professed to be indifferent. He hadn't run to become famous. All he wanted was sufficient money and recognition to continue living the life of an athlete for as long as possible. Before Munich, he was an oddball, a skinny guy who ran instead of getting a real job. After Munich, he was a champion, and that validated him in the eyes of plenty of people who thought *fartlek* was a dirty word. If it gave him more time to train, and excused his absences to his law school classmates and professors, he would take it. Anything to run.

But as much as he feigned indifference, he really did care what people thought. He put up a good façade, behind which even his own true feelings rarely emerged. He had learned this trick at an early age. To the outside world, he was the dutiful doctor's son, accompanying his father as he made his house calls. In his autobiography he would describe his feelings when his father drove 2,200 miles to join him at the celebration in Middletown: "When, to a standing ovation, my father was called by Lou Mills, 'One of the greatest humanitarians I have ever known,' I had tears in my eyes. I felt very close to my father then."

But Shorter harbored a secret that he wouldn't reveal for decades: as a boy, he was physically and emotionally abused by the very man whom everyone else saw as a lifesaver. His father, Dr. Samuel Shorter, regularly beat him and his siblings and raped two of his sisters.

Years later, in 2011, he would tell his story to *Runner's World* and in speaking engagements across the country: The late-night sounds of his father cross-examining his mother in the kitchen over some triviality. The resounding clomp of his shoes on the stairs. His heavy breathing in the doorway of the room. The alcohol on his breath. And then, worst of all, the sting of the belt across the boy's backside. His father's actions felt random, fueled by an irrational rage, and he was indiscriminate in his punishments. Any one of his children might suffer his wrath. When Frank was spared, he would have to listen quietly to the blows visited upon his siblings and to their groans. Trying to stop his father would, Frank quickly learned, only earn him a beating as well.

Running was his means of escape. He found solace in the routine, and the routine gave him a way to flee the thoughts that would otherwise ruin him. He shut out the pain with discipline and order and channeled it into the physical act of running. Running became an outlet for his fear and anger and a means to overcome them. For twenty-six miles at least, the brutal belt buckle in his father's raging hands was nothing compared to the brutal pace of a marathon.

Yet running was also a way to seek validation from his father and to please him, even though he never could. If his father berated the children for being lazy, Frank would work harder. If running made him a slacker, he would go to Yale. If winning the AAU championships was nothing, he would enroll in medical school. If a gold medal wasn't enough, he would earn a law degree.

Throughout Frank's childhood and collegiate career, his father never made it to a single race. He missed the Olympics because, he said, he didn't like to fly. He didn't watch the race on television because, he claimed, he was too nervous. When Frank won the marathon, his father remarked that it would give him a big head. Frank ran faster and faster, and still his father was unhappy.

The world record, however, eluded him. Perhaps if he broke it, he would finally earn his father's respect. Then he would not only be the fastest in the world; he would be the fastest of all time.

The Fukuoka Marathon was only five months after Munich. Shorter was already in shape and knew the course from his victory the previous year. Munich had been a tactical race on a twisting course, but Fukuoka was straight and fast: ideal conditions to challenge the world record. Although his training partners had moved on — Jack Bacheler to a postdoctoral fellowship and Jeff Galloway to a teaching job — Shorter returned to Gainesville and the Florida Track Club. He ran his miles on the roads and his intervals on the track, squeezing it all in around his classes, papers, and exams.

His law school classmates admired him, and some tried to emulate his efforts, if not his achievements. But many simply thought he was obsessive-compulsive or, worse, wasting his time. The university comprised mainly local students from middle- and working-class backgrounds. Some were the offspring of immigrants who had struggled to send their children to school. To them, spending valuable time out on the roads when he could have been studying seemed misguided, possibly deranged, certainly indulgent. They watched Frank pass by with a mixture of pride and concern but told themselves it was only his own future he was harming.

Shorter, however, was used to the strange looks and veiled condemnations. He had grown tired of explaining himself to the world. On the track, he was alone with his watch. On the roads, he ticked off miles like clockwork. He never missed a day, never slowed down. He was as constant as his father's moods were inconstant. If life was messy and unruly, running was measured and controlled. On the roads, he could take the lead, set the tempo, and no one could touch him.

But race day at Fukuoka was windier than Shorter had hoped, and although he hit thirteen miles on a world record pace, he slowed down in the second half of the race. He finished in 2:10:30, which was a new American mark but missed Derek Clayton's world record by about ninety seconds. It was a disappointment, but he minimized it. He told himself the marathon was not a sprint; it required patience and persistence, everything his father lacked. On the right course, with the right conditions, the record would fall.

With his law degree in hand, Shorter joined a firm in Boulder, Colorado, where he did part-time legal research and steered clear of clients. It was a perfect situation: it gave him some money, honed his marketable skills, and allowed him sufficient free time for training. There was no financial support for Olympic gold medalists in the marathon, and if he wanted to continue his attack on the world record, he would have to pay his own way. With the next Olympics more than a year away, he decided to sharpen his speed by running

5000- and 10,000-meter races. At the end of 1974, he was ranked tenth in the 5000. In the 10,000 he lost the number one ranking by one-tenth of a second to Brendan Foster of Great Britain in a race at London's Crystal Palace. His time of 27:46 was a personal best. (In those days, times were recorded only to the nearest tenth of a second. Shorter's personal best has since been reported as 27:45.91.) He was fast, hitting his peak, and nearly untouchable.

At the invitation of his friend Steve Prefontaine, he drove to Eugene with his wife and their dog to join Prefontaine in a race Pre had organized against the Finnish track team. Although Pre had failed to medal at the Olympics — taking the lead with a mile to go in the 5000 and battling Lasse Virén until fading to fourth — since then he had set American records in the two-mile, three-mile, 5000 meters, and 10,000 meters. He was a rock star, and fans in their GO PRE T-shirts followed him the way groupies followed the Grateful Dead. He was as extroverted as Shorter was introverted, as loquacious as Shorter was reticent. Shorter, older by four years, was the grizzled veteran, while Prefontaine was his heir apparent. They made an odd couple and at times seemed to have only a mustache in common. But both men were pragmatists dressed as idealists, were fiercely committed to the sport, and represented a resurgence in U.S. distance running.

Prefontaine was working for a new company named Nike, located in Beaverton, Oregon. He had run in a pair of the company's shoes at the 1972 Olympics and was the first runner paid by the company to market its brand. His job was to try to get other top runners to wear the shoes. On April 9, 1975, Prefontaine sent a letter with a pair of Nike Bostons to the unknown Bill Rodgers, who would use them twelve days later when he ran the Boston Marathon. The shoes were a half size too big, and the laces came untied during the race, but they were an improvement over what he was used to wearing.

Most running equipment at the time was barely better than the earliest shoe made of knotted sagebrush from the end of the last

Ice Age. In the mid-1800s, shoes were made on a single last and did not differentiate between the left foot and the right. In the 1890s, the company now known as Reebok pioneered the process of putting spikes on the bottom of leather shoes for racing, but the shoes were heavy and clumsy, and no good for training (although they did improve grip). Vulcanized rubber revolutionized footwear, as manufacturers began to use it for the soles of shoes called "sneaks" or "sneakers" (supposedly for how stealthy they made the wearer). In 1916, the U.S. Rubber Company began manufacturing sneakers it wanted to call Peds, but the word was already trademarked, so it settled on Keds. By the time of the 1936 Berlin Olympics, the brothers Adolf and Rudolf Dassler, who later founded Adidas and Puma, handcrafted running spikes for different-size feet and different running events. Jesse Owens, among other athletes, competed in their shoes.

In 1949, Kihachiro Onitsuka founded the Onitsuka Company, which produced Tiger basketball shoes, with distinctive octopus-like suction cups on their soles. (Onitsuka would later be acquired by ASICS.) Before long, Onitsuka was making Tiger running shoes, too, including the Mexico 66 and the Corsair. By 1970, according to a survey conducted by future *Runner's World* editor Joe Henderson, 70 percent of runners in the United States owned at least one pair of Tiger shoes, with Adidas the second most popular brand. Henderson's shoe diary, where he noted his own footwear, reflects the changing tastes of that time:

> 1970 — Tiger Boston, Lydiard Road Runner
> 1971 — Tiger Marathon
> 1972 — Tiger Marathon, Adidas Dragon
> 1973 — Tiger Boston, Tiger Marathon
> 1974 — Tiger Boston, Adidas Dragon, Tiger Jayhawk
> 1975 — Tiger Montreal
> 1976 — New Balance 320, New Balance 305

1977 — New Balance 305, Brooks Victor
1978 — Brooks Victor, Etonic Streetfighter, Brooks Vantage
1979 — Brooks Vantage, Brooks RT-1

Tiger's success in the United States was due in large part to Phil Knight. A mediocre middle-distance runner at the University of Oregon, Knight was a frequent guinea pig for coach Bill Bowerman, who liked to tinker with his athletes' shoes and even build his own. Bowerman was always looking for a way to shave a few ounces off a running shoe, knowing that over the course of a race, those ounces added up to many hundreds of pounds. He sawed apart various brands to see how they were constructed and experimented with different coverings, such as kangaroo and cod skin, to make the shoes lighter and more flexible.

After Knight graduated, he went to business school at Stanford, where, remembering Bowerman's quest for a better shoe, he wrote a paper titled "Can Japanese Sports Shoes Do to German Sports Shoes What Japanese Cameras Have Done to German Cameras?" His thesis was that a U.S. company could import inexpensive running shoes made overseas that would compete with Adidas in price. In 1962, he traveled to Japan, where he discovered the Tiger brand. He cajoled his way into a meeting with Onitsuka and struck a deal to become the distributor of Tiger shoes in the United States. He sent a pair to Bowerman, who offered to become his partner. With a handshake, the two men formed Blue Ribbon Sports. At first, they sold the shoes out of the trunk of Knight's car at track meets, but by 1967 they had their first retail store in Santa Monica, California.

Tiger shoes were good, but not as good as Adidas, and Bowerman was still looking for ways to make them better. He approached Onitsuka with various new designs that were incorporated into subsequent models. In 1972, he poured liquid urethane into his wife's waffle iron and invented the waffle sole, which was lighter and had a better grip than anything on the market. But Blue Ribbon's relationship with Onitsuka grew strained over the scope of the distributor-ship agreement and rights to the Corsair (or the Cortez, depending on who was selling it). Bowerman and Knight split from Onitsuka and renamed their company Nike. Soon the Nike Waffle Trainer was must-have equipment for the serious runner.

Although today it is fashionable to ignore the advances in foot-wear technology and to run barefoot, there is little evidence that running without shoes reduces injuries or increases performance. Barefoot runners take shorter strides, and the increased frequency of foot strikes results in the same cumulative impact on their body as shod runners who land on their heels. In addition, according to a recent study, barefoot running may increase "tensile stress within the plantar flexors" and "contact pressures on the metatarsals." In other words, running without cushioning hurts our feet and can lead to injuries. It may also make us slower. Researchers at the University of Colorado have concluded that running barefoot offers "no meta-bolic advantage over running in lightweight, cushioned shoes." In fact, the researchers discovered that for most participants in the study, "running in lightweight cushioned shoes was less metaboli-cally demanding than running barefoot, despite the greater mass." Even the Harvard biologist Daniel Lieberman, an early proponent of barefoot running, has acknowledged that "barefoot running is no panacea" for avoiding injuries.

Perhaps the strongest evidence against barefoot running, how-ever, is that elite athletes wear shoes. The drive to build a better shoe arose because a better shoe made a better runner. In the good old days, running on nothing, or next to nothing, hurt. As shoes improved, so did the ability to train harder and run faster. Today only a fool or a fanatic would train for a marathon in bare feet, and the number of elite athletes racing barefoot is exactly zero. Even famous former barefoot runners such as South Africa's Zola Budd switched to running in shoes because of recurring injuries. Kenyan and Ethiopian runners who grow up running barefoot because of economic necessity never go back once presented with their first pair of running shoes. They know, as do all elite athletes, that running barefoot puts them at a competitive disadvantage.

Both Prefontaine and Shorter were wearing their Nike Waffles to warm up before their 5000-meter race against the Finns. Pre had hoped to recruit Virén to run with them, but he dropped out at the last minute, claiming a leg injury (although he ran a 5000-meter race the very same day in Helsinki). Shorter was tired from the long drive and claimed not to be in shape. Yet when the gun was fired, he went to the front and took the lead during the first mile, running at a 4:17 pace. Prefontaine reeled him back in at the halfway mark, and then the two men pulled away from the pack, floating far out ahead. The crowd in the sold-out stadium rose to their feet. The sound of cheering was the loudest Shorter had ever heard and it spurred him on. But Prefontaine was a 3:54 miler, headstrong and as tough as nails. He wasn't going to let Shorter beat him on his home track, where he had never lost a race longer than a mile. He found another gear and ticked off three successive quarter-miles in 63, 64, and 63 seconds. He finished in 13:23.8, only 1.6 seconds slower than his U.S. record. After the race, the two men embraced, and Shorter hid his disappointment. It was Pre's race, after all; Shorter was just the marquee name and pacesetter. For thirteen minutes, however, he wanted to win.

After the race, Pre drove Shorter to a party, where they talked passionately about purging the sport of the hypocritical distinction between amateurs and professionals. Shorter would soon be investigated by the AAU following his testimony before the President's Commission on Olympic Sports in which he stated that he was a "professional." With the assistance of his law firm, he beat back the inquiry. But he was agitated by the inquisition, and it radicalized him. Soon the AAU found its match in the articulate young lawyer. He took up the charge and challenged the organization's control of track and field. This eventually led to the passage of the Amateur Sports Act of 1978, which established the U.S. Olympic Committee and removed the AAU from its governing role in the sport.

Prefontaine, however, would not live to see these changes. On May 30, 1975, just two minutes after dropping Shorter off at Kenny Moore's house following the party, he lost control of his convertible, crashed into a rock wall, and died.

Bill Rodgers in his hand-lettered GBTC T-shirt,
winning his first Boston Marathon.

Boston Globe via Getty Images

7

Boston Billy (1974–1975)

> When I won my first Boston, I didn't even know what I was
> training for. I just kept running longer and longer.
> — JOAN BENOIT SAMUELSON

B ILL RODGERS'S WIN at Falmouth in 1974 did not make
him a celebrity. Far from it. Besides getting his name wrong,
the mainstream media was not particularly interested in the
winner of a local road race. Shorter had put distance running on
the cover of *Sports Illustrated,* and Prefontaine had imbued it with
romance, but for most people it was still a sport for malnourished,
unathletic hippies.

Rodgers returned to his loops around Jamaica Pond and his day
job. He subsisted mostly on peanut butter and pizza and didn't have
enough money to buy decent running clothes. In September, he
completed his first New York City Marathon, circling Central Park
four times along with several hundred other hopefuls. He led by
three minutes through twenty-one miles, but then his legs cramped
up, and he faded to fifth. "Not enough long distance training," he
wrote in his log. "From now on, once a week a 20–25 mile run is

mandatory!!" New York was just a blip on the road race circuit, and Central Park a denuded wasteland overrun by pigeons and gangs. For his fifth-place finish, Rodgers didn't even earn a toaster.

Locally, however, he had begun to establish himself. He won the New England AAU fifteen-kilometer championship in Manchester, New Hampshire, and then a month later the NEAAU six-mile cross-country championship in Boston's Franklin Park. His mileage increased, and, at Coach Squires's urging, so did his interval training. He ran repeat miles or three-quarter miles at a pace of 4:40 to 4:50 per mile, with a two-minute recovery between them. He hated the work, but he knew it was the only way to get faster. In the afternoon, he would do an "easy" run of ten to eighteen miles. Several times that fall, his mileage went over 30 miles a day; his weekly average was around 120 and as high as 151.

It had now been about eighteen months since he'd resumed serious running. On December 1, 1974, he had his first breakthrough, winning the Philadelphia Marathon. His time was not particularly fast (2:21:57), but it was good enough for a course record and came on a cold, rainy day. It gave him renewed confidence after his failures in Boston and New York. As December drew to a close, he went for a couple of long runs with his friend Tommy Leonard: sixteen miles around Boston College and twelve miles down the Charles River. Molasses moved faster than Tommy, but Bill didn't mind. He enjoyed Tommy's stories, and later each day he went for another twelve-mile run at a much quicker pace. Tommy was a welcome distraction from the New Year's blues, and he kept Bill's mind from descending into gloom and self-doubt.

His GBTC teammates also supported him, and he relished his biweekly workouts on the Tufts indoor track. In their presence, he was not a barely employed janitor, but the best among a team of highly competitive athletes. Men such as Jack Fultz, Randy Thomas, and Bob Hodge would rule the New England running scene for most of the decade. But Rodgers's potential was already evident, and his early victories marked him as the runner to watch. Coach Squires pushed Rodgers in the workouts and urged him to run the U.S. trials for the world cross-country championship in Gainesville. Rodgers needed little convincing. The weather in Boston was, as he put it, as "cold as a farty New England dog shit day can be." Florida would be a welcome change of scenery.

Four days before the race, Rodgers came down with a 101-degree fever, which left him "spacey and sick." On February 9, 1975, however, the fever broke and his strength returned. The temperature outside was a dry 65 degrees, perfect for restoring the spirit.

The country's best distance runners gathered at the starting line, led by the world's number-one-ranked marathoner, Frank Shorter. It was actually the second meeting between the two men; the first occurred when Wesleyan raced against Yale in a meet won by Amby Burfoot. Rodgers, of course, knew Shorter and remembered their college contest. To Shorter, however, Rodgers didn't even exist; he was just another competitor to be trounced on the course. When Rodgers took the lead midway through the race, Shorter didn't worry. He bided his time and then came powering back on the latter part of the course, winning by fourteen seconds. Rodgers finished in a tie for third, which qualified him for the U.S. team that would travel to Morocco for the world championship. Coach Squires was ecstatic and took full credit for having convinced his charge to make the journey south. Rodgers let him gloat.

Back in Boston, Rodgers stepped up his training, running 157 miles, 124 miles, and 148 miles in the three weeks before traveling overseas. Then it was off to Rabat, Morocco. Unlike the Olympics, where running talent is spread across six different events, the world cross-country championship is a single race where marathoners compete with milers. Among runners, it is probably the most prestigious distance event. In the race that day was John Walker, the great miler from New Zealand, as well as Olympic bronze medalist Ian Stewart and Shorter.

Rodgers should have been intimidated, but he wasn't. He had enough miles under his belt that he felt prepared. He also knew that the day after having a fever, he had pulled ahead of Shorter on the Gainesville cross-country course. True, he fell back over the final hills, but it proved to him that Shorter was not invincible. In better health and on a different day, he could take him down. For his part, Shorter was not concerned about his American teammates. He had won the trials easily and was running well. Instead, he focused on the Europeans and the New Zealanders, who he believed were the men to beat.

Race conditions in Morocco were ideal: dry and not too warm. Rodgers felt terrific. True to form, he had forgotten his racing shoes, but teammate Gary Tuttle lent him a pair that fit perfectly. Rodgers went out fast and took the lead early, never looking back for Shorter. He ran aggressively, attacking the uphills and accelerating on the downhills. In the end, he held on for third place, the highest finish ever by an American in this race. Shorter finished more than a minute behind him in twentieth place.

Although the cross-country championship was too obscure to gather much press in the United States, Rodgers's first victory over Shorter heralded a sea change in U.S. distance running. Suddenly, the gold medalist was not alone at the top of the pyramid. Rodgers had "come from nowhere," as Shorter described it, an unknown who had bested a world champion. Shorter was still the more accomplished runner and still, to Rodgers, the more intimidating, but now it was a road race.

Coasting on the fumes of his victory, Rodgers returned to the States, where he finished second in the national thirty-kilometer road championships. He probably would have won, but he succumbed to an upset stomach, the bane of many runners' existence, and was forced to make a pit stop in the woods. Then it was back to Boston and "wind & slush & dog shit New England weather."

Up to this point, Rodgers was a runner's runner. His race in Morocco clearly established him as the real thing, but he could have gone on winning obscure distance races for the rest of his life and had little impact on the national consciousness. And that would have been fine with him. He did not expect any greater glory outside the cloistered world of running fanatics. He did not know there was an entire movement trailing in his footsteps, cold and weary, yearning to bust free, tired of being sprayed with slush in the breakdown lane, cursed at by kids and elderly people swerving around them. But all that was to change on April 21, 1975.

Winning a race requires more than good training. It requires good timing and good fortune. A runner who wakes up with a head cold on the morning of a big race is out of luck. He can't control a virus, nor can he dictate the weather, the road conditions, or who decides to suit up at the last minute. Running is not soccer, or football, or baseball, where half the players on the field are victorious. There can be only one winner. Everyone else is a loser.

When Rodgers awoke on the morning of the seventy-ninth running of the Boston Marathon, he knew God had smiled on him. He hated snow, but he also hated heat. The weather that morning was fit for Goldilocks: neither too hot nor too cold. There was a nice tailwind on the course and a chill in the air. Rodgers laced up the Nike Bostons that Prefontaine had sent him and slipped on a white T-shirt. His girlfriend, Ellen Lalone, had used a Magic Marker to write GBTC on the front of the shirt. The race was not until noon, so he had pancakes for breakfast and read the morning papers. He had run the course a hundred times and taken it apart with Coach Squires about as often, but his strategy was simple: he intended "to go like a bat out of hell and never stop or look back."

And that he did. England's Ron Hill was the favorite and course record holder. The Canadian Jerome Drayton was the man to watch. Rodgers dropped Hill early in the race, and at the fifteen-kilometer mark, it was Rodgers and Drayton. He heard a spectator cheering for Drayton, and it pissed him off — "a Boston spectator rooting for a Canadian" — so he poured it on. By the time Rodgers hit the series of climbs known as Heartbreak Hill, he was alone in front. His new shoes came loose, and he stopped once to tie them. He also stopped four times to drink water, because, as he explained, he couldn't drink and run at the same time. This amazed the spectators and the media, who couldn't believe the leader would simply come to a complete stop five times during a race. Nevertheless, he broke Ron Hill's course record by thirty-five seconds and Frank Shorter's U.S. record by the same amount, becoming the first American to run under 2:10 in the marathon. His time of 2:09:55 was the fifth-fastest marathon time in the world — ever.

When told he had broken the course record, Rodgers said that was "ridiculous" and "absurd"; he couldn't run that fast. From another runner, it might have sounded like false modesty, but the truth was that Rodgers had not paid close attention to his split times along the course, and in any event math was not his best subject. Coach Squires, of course, knew precisely how fast Rodgers had run, but he was no less amazed by the course record (although he professed not to be). As for Ellen, the time was just a number, but she would soon come to learn what it meant to the world and how it would change their lives.

When Frank Shorter heard the news in Colorado, he claimed he was not surprised, given Rodgers's performance at the world cross-country championship. This wasn't entirely true. Rodgers had proved himself to be a capable runner in Morocco, but no one could have foreseen that he would break the U.S. record and run under 2:10. In truth, it stung Shorter to lose his record to the unknown Rodgers. Although they were the same age, Shorter was the elder statesman of American distance running and Rodgers the callow interloper. It was like having a meticulously constructed sandcastle torn down by a bumbling kid — one who couldn't even afford a pair of sneakers that fit. Shorter chalked up the new record to a favorable tailwind and Boston's downhill course, but he began plotting his revenge.

As for Rodgers, he joined his teammates and coach at the Eliot Lounge, where Tommy Leonard poured Blue Whales and beer, and the jukebox played his victory song.

Bill Rodgers leads Frank Shorter during the early part of the race
in their first meeting at Falmouth.

Courtesy Charlie Rodgers

8

Showdown at Noon (1975)

I always felt he was more preoccupied with me than I was with him.
— FRANK SHORTER ON BILL RODGERS

Frank was a master at the psychological game.
— BILL RODGERS ON FRANK SHORTER

RODGERS'S VICTORY AT BOSTON put Falmouth on the map. No longer was he the unknown "Will Rogers" who had somehow managed to beat America's star miler, Marty Liquori, in an odd distance race. He was the winner of the oldest and most venerated marathon in the United States and the new American record holder. With his blue eyes, impish grin, and sandy blond hair, he became an instant media favorite. In contrast to the cerebral Shorter and the glowering Salazar, Rodgers's guilelessness endeared him to the press, making him the perfect spokesman for the nascent running movement. By dint of association, Falmouth basked in his reflected glory.

Tommy Leonard couldn't have been happier. The Eliot Lounge

was now the official watering hole of the Boston Marathon and the American record holder, Bill Rodgers. The GBTC was the hottest running club in the United States. Coach Squires was elevated from guru to deity. And the beer flowed like, well, wine. These were heady days in the Boston running community, making everyone involved feel as if he was at the hub of a wheel that had begun to spin rapidly, showering pixie dust on all who were near — the kind that made runners fly.

Yet something was missing. As Leonard, Rich Sherman, and John Carroll began planning for the third Falmouth Road Race, Frank Shorter's absence was palpable. Shorter was tearing up the roads at the non-marathon distances, and the course record at Falmouth was held by the man who had broken Shorter's marathon record. It made perfect sense that Shorter would want to challenge Rodgers at Falmouth — at least to the three men trying to plan the event. But Shorter seemed to have other things on his mind.

In Charleston, West Virginia, in a race inaugurating the National Track and Field Hall of Fame, Shorter got his first crack at the newly emergent Rodgers by beating him soundly in a two-mile race. But neither man took the race particularly seriously, given the circumstances and the distance. It was barely long enough to warm up their muscles and certainly not in either man's wheelhouse. Ten days later, Rodgers ran a 31.6-kilometer race in Puerto Rico during which he became "sick from heat prostration el vomit & el diareah!" Even so, he managed to win and got "a nice huge trophy to sell! & a case of good rum."

Rodgers loved a party. He also loved Tommy Leonard and would have done almost anything for him. Tommy was more than a favorite bartender and an occasional (albeit slow) running partner. He was everything that was special about the sport of running: an ordinary guy who mingled with the elite then partied with the best of them. Running had no locker rooms that were closed to the press, no agents (at least not then), and no bloated contracts that encouraged sloth and ennui. The only prima donnas were the AAU officials. That was the charm, and in some respects would be the downfall, of the sport. In 1975, a bowlegged bartender could prevail on the American record holder in the marathon to place a call to another champion and convince him to come to an obscure town on Cape Cod to run a race from bar to bar that wasn't even measured correctly.

Shorter was on his way to Europe to run the track circuit, but Rodgers passed along Tommy's invitation anyway. He knew Shorter would be "tough as hell," and to a certain extent he hoped Frank wouldn't show up. Later, he would joke that Tommy had forced the invite on him. But the truth was, Rodgers relished the rivalry. Road racing was about "taking down kings," and Shorter was still the sovereign. Besides, it wasn't as if Rodgers was giving up a payday by inviting Shorter to compete. He already had a toaster and didn't need another T-shirt.

Although Shorter came to be associated with Gainesville and Boulder, he was a son of New England, and he knew Woods Hole from several trips to Martha's Vineyard with a family friend. The race intrigued him, as did the chance to take on the man who had wrested away his marathon record. He accepted Tommy's invitation with just one condition; he wanted to be paid what he received for running the 10,000 meters on the track: a whopping $600. There was also the cost of flying him in from Colorado for the race. For that, Tommy turned to businessman Bill Crowley, who owned the Captain Kidd and the Oar & Anchor in Falmouth. Crowley told Tommy to come back and see him when he was sober, but Tommy persisted, and eventually Crowley agreed to underwrite Shorter's trip and put him up at his home in Falmouth. As an added incentive, Tommy got a local business to donate a television to give to Shorter.

News of Shorter's appearance spread quickly in the small communities of Woods Hole and Falmouth. The *Falmouth Enterprise* predicted that 650 runners would show up to run; more than 800 did, double the previous year's number. At least 150 registered at the last minute, crowding the recreation center and creating a chaotic scene, as the *Enterprise* reported: "runners with sweat pants, runners with shorts and tee shirts bearing the name of a track club, track clubs, sneaker manufacturers, track shoes of vibrant blue, red, yellow, some with sneakers [*sic*]." On race day in Woods Hole, according to the newspaper, "Water Street looked like Rio at Carnival time or Paris on Bastille day. People lined the sidewalks. Spectators hung out of windows. A large group was seated atop the tower-like roof behind the Fishmonger Café."

If the newspaper was prone to hyperbole (and syntactical errors), it could be forgiven its enthusiasm. Rarely had so many people in the United States come together in one place to participate in a sporting event. Fans gathered to *watch;* they didn't gather to *play.* It went against Americans' preconceived notion of sports, which involved teams or competitors locked in combat. Even Frank Shorter had never seen an event with so many participants. In his marathons, there were never more than a hundred competitors; on the track, no more than a dozen. The race was a "happening," according to the *Boston Globe,* a lovefest dedicated to the sport of running. For Tommy, it was a way to "bring together in these troubled times."

But the size of the field and the growing inexperience of some of the participants led to stern warnings from race organizers. Dr. Charles Montgomery, who had treated heat stroke victims the year before, cautioned that "last year's race was not achieved without serious medical strain on several individuals." He noted that six runners were brought to the emergency room, and two were hospitalized overnight. "Both were psychotic. One did not become rational for 36 hours. Both were adult athletic males, in their young 20's in excellent physical condition." His dire warning, reflective of the breathless naïveté of that moment, was ignored.

Town officials were more concerned about the number of runners and the strain on public resources. As an accommodation, race directors Carroll and Sherman agreed to move the finish line 180 yards farther down the road past the Brothers Four. This meant the race would end on a downhill, rather than a sharp climb. More important, it provided easy access to the Falmouth Heights ballpark, so that finishers could be ushered quickly away from the finish line and onto the grassy field. The course was now announced as 7.4 miles — instead of 7.3 — although both those distances would turn out to be incorrect. The race was officially sanctioned by the AAU, but that didn't mean it was measured accurately. In those days, measuring a course usually meant driving its length in a car or, at best, riding its length on a bicycle with a pedometer. It was not until 1987 that a formal standard and practice for measuring racecourses was adopted, which required, among other things, that the certifier measure the shortest distance between points — usually a tangent — rather than the way a runner might actually approach it (hugging a curve, for example, instead of cutting across it). The Falmouth course was remeasured in 2007 by Jim Gerweck, editor at large for *Runner's World,* and officially certified as 7.0 miles.

To get to Falmouth, Shorter flew in to Logan Airport in Boston. Tommy asked a friend who was a state trooper to pick up Shorter in his police cruiser. Shorter's hair was more unruly than in Munich, and his mustache seemed larger, but he was easily recognizable as the thinnest and fittest person in the terminal. They drove down to Cape Cod with the lights flashing. When they arrived, John Carroll was waiting to greet Shorter with the television set. This didn't seem right to the business owner who had donated it — Shorter hadn't even run yet, he protested — but the gift was for showing up, not winning. Technically, the gift violated amateur rules, but it was a common ruse to get around the prohibitions against awarding prize money. It could be sold for cash, and the AAU would be none the wiser. (Shorter's $600 appearance fee, however, was clearly a violation of the rules.) After stashing his gift, Shorter checked in at the Crowleys', put on his shorts, and jogged the course.

Although Tommy Leonard was not a sophisticated man, he had a runner's intuition. "Bar to bar" was just a sales pitch. The course from Woods Hole to Falmouth Heights, on the other hand, was the real thing. As Shorter jogged the route, he noticed it was naturally divided into three segments: the woods and hills of the first three miles; the flats along Surf Drive and Falmouth Harbor; the last mile into the Heights. Unlike the uniformity of a track, the course threw different challenges at the runners at different points. A man could run the hills hard, only to wilt in the sun along the beach. He could hang back in the hills but lose the thread of the leaders by the flats. It was a course of exploration as well as physical beauty, and each turn brought a new discovery: lighthouse, salt marsh, beach, boatyard, ball field. The elite runners were not racing for the scenery, of course, but the backdrop was both challenging and inspirational. The varied terrain forced minute changes in pacing and strategy, and Shorter took the measure of each step as he anticipated the contest ahead.

After his run, he was off to the Oar & Anchor, where race organizers had arranged a press conference with the *Falmouth Enterprise, Boston Globe,* and *Boston Phoenix.* Shorter sat with Rodgers at the front of the bar answering questions from a handful of reporters, while race volunteers and bar patrons looked on. A reporter asked Shorter if he was worried about anyone else in the field. "Realistically, the race is a contest between him and me," he said, nodding at Rodgers. He didn't discount the possibility, however, of "some little skinny guy" breaking out of the pack and trying for the lead. He said this in a way that indicated he wasn't worried about losing the race to the "skinny guy"; he just didn't want the skinny guy to mess with his pacing. There was no one in the United States, except perhaps Rodgers, who could beat Shorter at this distance.

Rodgers found Shorter cool and not particularly friendly. They'd grown up within a hundred miles of each other, but Shorter was a track man who trained in Colorado and Florida, while Rodgers was Boston Billy, a road runner through and through. Rodgers was naturally affable, while Shorter was guarded and calculating, and he kept Rodgers guessing. Few people who knew Shorter remembered his warmth. (According to a friend, once while he was running with his girlfriend, she stumbled and fell, and rather than helping her up, he simply told her to watch herself.) But he was the best distance runner in the world, and he saw no reason to cozy up to anyone. In part, this was a strategy. "I always wanted Bill to be thinking about me," he later said. It was the same strategy he'd employed at the Olympics: as the leader, he forced his competitors to waste energy trying to guess his next move while he dictated the pace. But it didn't endear him to Rodgers or the other athletes.

Shorter finished his beer and went back to the Crowleys' to retire. Rodgers was staying with John and Lucia Carroll. He planned to rise early and skip breakfast. Both men slept lightly, tossing and turning and dreaming of the road.

The morning broke gray and misty, with an unusual headwind along Surf Drive. Not ideal conditions for Shorter, who didn't like the rain, but at least the danger of heat exhaustion was minimized. In the recreation center, John Carroll and Rich Sherman dealt with the last-minute crush of entrants, for which they blamed Tommy Leonard. In his enthusiasm, Leonard had encouraged late sign-ups and promised the resources to handle them. But no one was prepared for 150 race-day applications, the questions that accompanied them, or making change for an endless stream of twenty-dollar bills. To add confusion to the madness, there were rented buses lined up outside to drive runners to Woods Hole, and someone had to usher people onto them, deal with the complaints of those who couldn't fit, and politely reject the entreaties of freeloaders who just needed a lift. As it was, the last bus arrived late, and the start time had to be pushed back to accommodate it.

Rodgers's strategy was the same as at Boston: go out hard, maintain, kick. By this point, he was no longer in awe of Shorter and knew he could beat him. But he was also realistic: between the two men, Shorter had the greater leg speed. Rodgers's best chance was to force the pace early and hope the burn in Shorter's muscles would take its toll in Falmouth Heights. Even the best-trained runner could not defeat biochemistry, which dictated that at some point, the buildup of lactic acid would exceed the body's ability to utilize it and lead to a lowering of muscle cell pH, resulting in pain and fatigue. The only way to eliminate excess lactic acid was to slow down or stop. (Slowing down removes lactic acid faster than stopping, which is why coaches suggest a cooldown after a long run.)

Shorter, for his part, didn't discount Rodgers's triumph in the world cross-country championship, but he knew that Bill was not a 10,000-meter runner. He attributed his failure to beat Rodgers at the cross-country championship to a stomach cramp. Besides, Falmouth was three miles shorter, a road race, and relatively flat, favoring Shorter's smooth, efficient stride. His strategy was to let Rodgers set the early pace, not lose contact, then outkick him.

Neither man's strategy was a surprise to the other. But sports strategies rarely are. A football team with an excellent offense will emphasize its running game, while its opponent will focus on the sack and blitz. A tennis player with a powerful serve will concentrate on the serve and volley, while his opponent will try to keep him on the baseline by hitting deep. To do anything else would be counterproductive and a waste of resources. The baseline player may try to rush the net occasionally, but he can't hide his weakness or pretend he's a different athlete. Surprise works only when it's limited and focused: a single punch, a last-second punt, a fadeaway jump shot. Most sporting contests are won or lost on execution over the length of the game.

Now, as 810 runners lined up in front of the Captain Kidd, all of them were thinking about what they needed to do to execute. Some just hoped to finish, viewing seven miles as an end in itself. But most had a specific goal in mind: a six-minute pace, beating last year's time, outkicking their neighbors. Most were familiar with the course and knew what they had to do to achieve their goal. Most would fail.

A successful strategy requires a keen awareness of one's strengths and weaknesses and a constant reevaluation during the sporting event itself. The runner who thinks he can maintain a six-minute pace over the course of seven miles, but who has only been running twenty miles a week, is deceiving himself. In running, this kind of self-deception is rampant. It may be because the beginning of a race feels so easy, and most runners tend to go out too fast. It may also be because runners are eternal optimists, always convinced they can achieve a new personal best. Few would withstand the pain if they thought there would be no reward. Part of what makes an elite runner great, however, is the ability to balance that optimism with pragmatism, to be aware of his limitations even as he tries to exceed them. Too much confidence leads to failure; too little, the same.

So when the gun went off and Rodgers bolted into the lead, he was confident his training and racing had prepared him for his strategy. He ran at a pace he believed reasonable based on the intervals and hill work Coach Squires had prescribed. His legs automatically fell into a rhythm, muscle memory taking over, strides quick and clipped and brisk.

They hit the first mile in 4:45, somewhere between the pace Rodgers had run in the two-mile against Shorter and the pace he'd run in the Boston Marathon. It was slower than the previous year's pace, but Rodgers was not concerned. Then, he'd been chasing Liquori, who had gone out too fast, his inexperience triumphing over common sense. Once the lactic acid overwhelmed his muscles, he had to slow down to reabsorb it. That was when Rodgers, who had a much better sense of pacing on the roads, easily outmatched him.

Shorter, however, was no Liquori. He kept Rodgers within a stride. The two men ran together, but not side by side. Rodgers went down the hill, and Shorter went down with him, but along a different tangent. To the spectator, it seemed as if the two men were running different races, each unaware of the other's presence. Their

103

eyes looked straight ahead, never to the side or behind them. But their ears were keenly attuned to the other man's breathing, and in their peripheral vision they sensed each other's presence.

Rodgers hit the second mile in 4:42, executing perfectly. He was neither too fast nor too slow. With the twisting, narrow roads and the staccato rhythm of the short hills, Shorter struggled to keep contact. He preferred to be the one dictating the pace and was uncomfortable in Rodgers's shadow. But Rodgers kept pushing, not easing up as they passed F. R. Lillie and Fay Roads, then climbed the small hill before the beach.

There is a moment in every race when the tide turns. It occurs when fatigue overwhelms the brain's ability to keep urging the body onward. A rival attacks, and the runner cannot respond. The moment is both physical and psychological, determined as much by the inability of cells to keep up with the demand for energy as by the central nervous system's determination that enough is enough. Where does will yield to chemistry? When does passion yield to reason?

Rodgers and Shorter came down the hill with the salt marsh to their right. Rodgers still held a small lead, but he had failed to shake Shorter in the woods. Now as they approached the beach, he could only hope the strain of the early miles had taken the life out of Shorter's legs. The wind buffeted them, and a gray mist settled like a shroud. Rodgers fought to maintain his form, knowing that every asynchronous arm movement or head bob was a waste of energy. He drove forward on the balls of his feet, knees knocking and shoulders hunched.

But as the road flattened, Shorter felt back in control. The beach extended before them, and it gave him a sprinter's sense of power, as if he could just dash down the road, leaving everything in his wake. This was the moment to see what Rodgers still had. In a quarter-mile stretch, he opened a ten-yard lead. By the four-mile mark, he was two full strides in front. The narrow beach along Surf Drive was crowded with spectators. They lined the roads and filled the wooden beach cabanas that had been transformed into road race party shacks. Although they cheered Shorter's arrival, they exhorted Rodgers to catch him. Shorter may have had an Olympic medal, but Boston Billy had their hearts.

Rodgers, however, could not respond. The race was not over, but the momentum had clearly changed. Now Rodgers's only hope was to maintain his pace and hope that Shorter made his move too early. Rodgers was not going to run any faster, but it was possible Shorter would slow down. In fact, they had run their fourth mile in 4:49, the slowest one yet. Shorter's burst of speed was really just a return to their earlier pace. What appears to most spectators as one runner pouring it on is usually his competitors running out of gas. This might have been good news for Rodgers, except it was he who was fading.

By the five-mile mark, Shorter had increased his lead another ten yards. Now it was a race to the finish line. As at the Olympics, Shorter just had to keep his pace. As for Rodgers, he had lost a stride or two, but he was not done yet. By slowing down another five seconds, his body was able to partially recover. For most people, running a single mile at a five-minute pace would be impossible. For Bill Rodgers, it gave him a breather and allowed him to consider trying to catch Shorter.

But Shorter wasn't about to let that happen. He looked back, saw that Rodgers had fallen twenty yards behind, and knew that now was the time to bury him. There was still a slender filament connecting the two runners, and Shorter aimed to snap it. So he attacked again, and soon he had forty yards. By Grand Avenue, entering Falmouth Heights, he had almost disappeared over the rise in the road. Now Rodgers was broken. He knew he wouldn't be able to make up the distance. He looked behind him to make sure no one was gaining and resigned himself to second place.

Shorter reached the water, then made a sharp left into the final climb. The wind blew hard, but he ran harder — up the hill and past the front doors of the Casino and the Brothers Four. The crowd pushed into the road, held back by a thin rope, leaving a narrow passage only two or three runners wide. Shorter threaded the channel and drove toward the tape, where Rich Sherman, John Carroll, and Tommy Leonard stood beaming. He raised his arms, the orange FLORIDA on his singlet catching the light, and then he crossed the finish line. The time was 33:24, breaking Rodgers's course record by fifty-two seconds.

Rodgers followed about a hundred yards behind, also faster than his previous year's time. It would be nearly another two minutes before the third-place finisher arrived.

Photographers and press rushed the winner, but Shorter refused to stand for a picture until he found Rodgers and shook his hand. Then the two men posed politely for photographs and spoke with the press as the rest of the field began to stream into the Heights. Shorter had won this round, but Rodgers wasn't about to concede the fight. Today, Shorter was the better runner. Tomorrow, Rodgers would be back on Commonwealth Avenue with Coach Squires and the GBTC, pounding the hills.

The medal ceremony followed the race, and Tommy handed out prizes on a makeshift wooden platform, posing for photos with his two champions like a proud mother. It was a glorious finish to a beautiful dream. Three years after watching Shorter cross the finish line in Munich, Tommy's crazy, improbable wish had come true. He felt the warm glow of the race in his belly (or maybe it was the beer). Shorter's presence was like a palliative for a hard-luck life, and although he was not a man who ever felt sorry for himself, the boy who ran away from the orphanage allowed himself a few tears of joy. This was what he lived for: the camaraderie of the running life. It was the family he'd never had, the embrace of eight hundred souls sharing his reverie.

Then he was back to recruiting, soliciting promises from both men to return for next year's race. There were many miles between this summer and next, with a stopover in Montreal for the Olympic

Games, but Tommy grinned like a leprechaun and told his charges he would hold them to their word.

The party at the Brothers Four was already in full swing. Fifteen hundred glasses of beer would be served, as well as countless bowls of clam chowder. The food line stretched from the kitchen all the way through the dining room and into the front hall. Friends and family crowded inside, and those who couldn't fit spilled down the hill and onto the ball field.

The two honored guests, however, were nowhere to be found. Frank Shorter and Bill Rodgers slipped out of the party and together jogged the seven miles back to Woods Hole.

Frank Shorter shaking hands with Waldemar Cierpinski
after the 1976 Olympic marathon.

Associated Press

9

Cheaters Prosper (1976)

What Frank and Abebe [Bikila] did, they did without drugs.
— BILL RODGERS

As LONG AS THERE has been sport, there has been cheating.

In the ancient Olympics, competitors ate exotic meats that supposedly gave them strength. Before chromosome testing, the Greeks competed naked to prevent women from pretending to be men. In 1807, Abraham Wood claimed that he used laudanum to stay awake for twenty-four hours while racewalking against the great Captain Barclay. In the 1904 Olympic marathon, the American Thomas J. Hicks downed several doses of strychnine and egg whites, followed by a large glass of brandy, given to him by his "trainer," Charles Lucas. Although he finished second, he was declared the winner when it was discovered that the first-place finisher, Fred Lorz, had been driven in a car for at least three miles. The race had been run in 90-degree heat on a road that was so dusty one runner suffered a near-fatal hemorrhage from breathing difficulties. It didn't help that twenty automobiles kept pace with the runners, kicking up rocks and dirt the entire way. When Hicks begged for water during the race, Lucas refused, giving him a sponge bath with water warmed by the car's radiator instead. Afterward, Lucas bragged that "the marathon race, from a medical standpoint, demonstrated that drugs are of much benefit to athletes along the road."

But it was at the 1976 Olympics where rampant drug use became official state policy. Even before the games began, twenty-three U.S. athletes failed drug tests at the trials (although none were punished). Rumors swirled that Lasse Virén, who had completed the "double-double" in the 5000 and 10,000 meters, was blood doping, a process in which blood is withdrawn from the body and then hemoglobin is reinfused shortly before competition. The theory — since proven effective by cyclists in the Tour de France, who have accomplished the same thing with the drug EPO (erythropoietin) — is that more hemoglobin allows the body to work harder by bringing more oxygen to the muscles. Virén had run four races in eight days and announced he would run his first marathon the day after winning the 5000 meters, in an effort to equal the "triple" of Emil Zátopek in 1952. Although Virén has denied the allegations, many observers believed his attempt was possible only with the assistance of a biological boost.

Frank Shorter, however, was not worried about Virén. Indeed, he thought there was no one who could beat him if he stayed healthy and ran his race. He had lost both his number one ranking and his U.S. record to Bill Rodgers, but only because he had mostly abstained from longer races for a year. The Montreal Olympics was his chance to match the great Abebe Bikila's two gold medals in the marathon, and he knew history would judge him by this race. He quit his job to concentrate on training, while his wife, Louise, supported them because his running provided almost no income. The AAU questioned every travel reimbursement he received, and the Boston Athletic Association wouldn't even pay for him to fly to Boston to run the marathon. The couple spent the winter in Boulder with plastic over their windows because they couldn't afford storms.

For Bill Rodgers, the Olympics was his opportunity to prove himself in the marathon. There were still people who thought his record at Boston was a fluke, and at Fukuoka he finished third in a race won by Jerome Drayton. Since Falmouth, he had raced Shorter only once, a ten-miler in Lynchburg, Virginia, where they deliberately tied. It was Rodgers's idea as he pulled even with Shorter late in the race, but Shorter initially resisted it. A race was a race, and there could be only one winner. In the end, he agreed, realizing that refusing to do so would make him look petty and petulant. (Race officials awarded first place to Rodgers, however, because they could not record a tie.)

In truth, Rodgers was still a little in awe of Shorter and knew he was the less experienced contender. To train for the U.S. team, he awoke at 6 a.m. during the frozen Boston winter and ran on snow-narrowed streets, where cars could barely see him in the dark. At lunchtime he changed in a small bathroom in the basement of the school where he worked and snuck outside for a run while the kids lined up to eat. When he returned there was no place to shower, so he had to rinse off in the sink. His principal couldn't understand his compulsion and asked him why he didn't concentrate more on his "vocation rather than [his] avocation." This was the U.S. record holder in the marathon, yet most Americans found his sport puzzling and odd. Others felt threatened by it, seeing the vestiges of hippie free love and antiestablishmentarianism.

The boom was gaining momentum, yet it was still a time of anger and confusion. The country was reeling from two decades of military conflict in defense of ideals no one quite understood, while the economy stagnated and President Gerald Ford told New York City to drop dead. Angry bands such as U2, the Clash, and the Ramones all appeared on the scene; angry movies such as *Network* and *Taxi Driver* were released; and angry bombs erupted in Soweto, Argentina, Ireland, and London. There was little to cheer about, and even the cheering felt strained, like waving a flag while the floats broke down and veered off course.

But it was time for a party. The United States was two hundred years old, and what better way to celebrate than with Olympic gold? Overnight, it seemed, after the long drought, the U.S. had doubled its chances of winning the marathon, and possibly the other distance events as well. As its international influence waned, the country could at least console itself with its athletic prowess.

Alas, the Olympic coronation began inauspiciously. Montreal beat out Los Angeles for the summer games, and although Denver was awarded the winter games, Colorado reneged on its commitment because of rising costs. Instead, the Winter Olympics were held in Innsbruck, Austria.

For Shorter and Rodgers, however, Montreal was a much better venue for the marathon than Los Angeles. Running twenty-six miles in LA smog in July was nobody's idea of fun. (Years later, the same objections would be raised about Beijing and force the withdrawal of marathon world record holder Haile Gebrselassie.) Canada was a kinder, gentler version of the United States, where neither runner would have to face home field pressure to bring back a medal. Shorter claimed not to care about the weight of the expectations placed on him. As the favorite, he wrote, "the other runners watch you, perhaps more than they should. They think about you, perhaps more than they should. This helps you to control the race, to run your best while forcing others to contour their efforts to you."

First, however, both men had to qualify for the U.S. team. Because they were trying to qualify in the 10,000 meters as well as the marathon, there were two Olympic trials on two separate dates. In a nod to the marathon's difficulty, the qualifying race for it was held a month earlier than the 10,000-meter trials. But that still meant the runners were forced to run a competitive marathon and then *two* 10,000-meter races (a qualifying heat and a final), all before even getting to Montreal.

Ever since New Zealand coach Arthur Lydiard demonstrated during the 1960s that running and racing should be divided into periods of strength building, speed work, and then competition, elite runners have understood that "peaking" for a race is not a random event, but a carefully controlled and planned occurrence that can happen only with limited frequency. Peaks are not sustainable for more than a few weeks and take months to build. In an ideal world, a runner would spend a year building to one race and then execute at his top level of fitness. But that is simply not feasible in the real world, where the calendar is controlled by promoters, sponsors, officials, coaches, agents, agencies, and the runner's own need to prove himself and eke out a meager living. The competitive runner can't live in the lab. He must get out on the roads.

The marathon trials were held in Eugene, Oregon, on May 22, 1976. The weather was cool and windless, fairly ideal conditions for the distance. Shorter believed he was in the best shape of his life. Rodgers had run 157 miles a week for the three weeks leading up to the trials. He was also in terrific shape, but he had not given himself adequate time to recover from his high mileage. Eleven thousand fans filled the stadium at Hayward Field to see the first meeting between the two runners in the marathon. Eugene was a running town, and Steve Prefontaine's ghost haunted it. Even if the rest of America did not understand the sport, those gathered to watch knew they were witnessing a historic moment.

The two men went out together in the lead and had drawn away from the rest of the pack by the halfway point. According to Shorter, he "would've settled for a tie," but Rodgers began to feel the effects of his hard training, with his calves cramping and tightening. The top three men would make the Olympic team, and if Shorter had really wanted a tie, he could have slowed down and still easily qualified. Indeed, some sportswriters noted that he appeared to be accelerating near the end and looking over his shoulder. But whether from a legitimate fear that he would be overtaken or because he wanted to avoid the ignominy of Lynchburg (where a tie had earned him second place), Shorter cruised to victory in 2:11:51, seven seconds ahead of Rodgers.

One month later, the two men returned to Hayward Field to run qualifying heats in the 10,000 meters. Rodgers won his heat with a personal best of 28:32.7, and Shorter won his in 28:33.6, beating Craig Virgin by one-hundredth of a second. In the finals, three days later, Shorter won in 27:55.4, with Virgin four seconds behind, followed by Garry Bjorklund and then Rodgers, in 28:04.4.

That Shorter could win the marathon and then return and beat track star Virgin in the 10,000 meters was a tribute to his fitness and versatility. Running the 10,000 on a track with a pack of other runners is an entirely different race than running 26.2 miles on the road. For one thing, the 10,000 consists of twenty-five laps around a flat, uniform 400-meter track, while the marathon is usually run on city streets with bridges, potholes, hills, and turns. The 10,000 is run in a tight pack of thirty or forty runners, all of whom are jockeying for position, trying not to get too far outside on the corners but also not wanting to get boxed in on the straightaways. In the marathon, the course is open and wide, and it's not really possible to get boxed in. The 10,000 is run in spikes on a rubber surface, while the marathon is run in racing flats on the road. Most important, the 10,000 requires more fast-twitch muscle fibers in order to run at a pace that averages around 4:30 per mile, with surges that are the equivalent of running a mile under four minutes. Although it's common for a sprinter to double in the 100 and 200 meters, or the 200 and 400 meters, it's unusual for a distance runner to master both the 10,000 and the marathon at the same time. The only runner to have won both events at the Olympics was the incomparable Emil Zátopek.

Yet Frank Shorter was now the U.S. Olympic trials champion in both the marathon and the 10,000 meters, and he was the clear favorite in the former for the Olympic Games. He might have been one of the favorites in the 10,000 as well, but an injury to his foot made him wary of doubling. Most important, he wanted to secure his place in history, which he knew meant the marathon. This gave Rodgers — as the fourth-place finisher — an opportunity to compete at 10,000 meters. But Rodgers also injured his foot on the track, and he would spend the next six weeks avoiding all speed work in the hope that it would heal. And so the fifth-place finisher at the Olympic trials, Ed Mendoza, became the third man on the Olympic 10,000-meter team.

Thus it was that the U.S. Olympic trials, in the name of fairness, compromised both Shorter's and Rodgers's chances at a medal by forcing them to run multiple races to qualify for the team. Both suffered injuries that had physiological as well as psychological effects, all in pursuit of a race that they ultimately chose not to run and in which they might not have medaled. By the time they arrived in Montreal, they were beat-up and battered, and neither was at his peak.

Shorter's plan for the marathon, as it had been at Munich, was to push the pace from the beginning and then try to separate himself from the other runners. But during his warm-up, the rubber soles of his running shoes separated from the fabric. Then, as he waited frantically for another pair, it began to rain. Shorter hated the feeling of being wet and uncomfortable on the road. It made him tighten up, and he believed it affected his form. His shoes arrived, but it continued to rain. So five minutes before the start of the race, as he hustled out to the track, he decided to hold back and run more conservatively.

Rodgers, meanwhile, had spent the past three days lying on his back in his room hoping the pain in his right metatarsus would disappear. But it still hurt, and the medical treatment he received was rudimentary and limited, which frustrated and angered him. As he later wrote, "It seems amazing that I, the athlete with the fastest qualifying time for my event, who was now limping around injured in the Olympic Village, was not given more assistance by the staff at Montreal." Despite the fact that these two men represented the United States' best chance for a medal in the non-sprint events, distance runners were the ungainly cousins of their bigger, more accomplished shorter-distance teammates. They were mostly on their own — in terms of training and care — and for better or worse, U.S. doctors were woefully ignorant about how to treat them.

So when Shorter and Rodgers toed the line at the start of the marathon, neither was 100 percent, and both were at a competitive disadvantage against some of the Eastern bloc athletes, who cheated with a scientific rigor and made U.S. efforts seem strictly for amateurs. But they were still champions: Shorter, the gold medalist in 1972 and the prohibitive favorite, and Rodgers with the fastest time in the world that year. The other runners eyed them warily and planned their strategies around them. When the gun went off, most of the serious contenders had them in their sights.

A pack of about twelve men quickly established themselves at the front. Along with Shorter and Rodgers, Jerome Drayton was there, as was Lasse Virén, and a runner from East Germany named Waldemar Cierpinski. Rodgers was near the front, while Shorter hung back, in keeping with his newly revised strategy. Virén's plan was to stick with Shorter as long as he could — "like a dolphin following a ship," he said. But Shorter played a game of hide-and-seek, in which he would drift back and put another runner between them. Then Virén would look around, slowing down until he found the American. When he did, Shorter would pick up the pace and move into the pack. At one water stop, the runners became separated, and Shorter raised an arm and waved to Virén as if to say, "Here I am." Although it may have appeared to be a gesture of camaraderie, it was a psychological ploy, signaling to Virén (and any others who might be watching) that he was fresh enough to toy with his competitors.

Meanwhile, Rodgers was struggling. By ten kilometers, he knew this wasn't going to be his race, not because his foot hurt — which it did — but because his lack of speed work as a result of the injury made it impossible for him to maintain the pace with the leaders for long. They were averaging about five minutes per mile, and the only way to feel comfortable at that pace is to run a lot of 4:40 miles in practice. No amount of distance can substitute for speed, because the heart, lungs, and muscles need to be trained to perform at their anaerobic threshold. Rodgers hadn't trained, and now he was suffering the consequences. Soon, he had fallen out of the lead pack.

Just before twenty kilometers, Shorter took off. He described it as "more of a sprint than a surge," intended to see who would come with him. It didn't break the field the way his move at Munich had; six men stayed with him. But around twenty-five kilometers, he surged again, and this time he dropped everyone except a runner he mistook for Carlos Lopes from Portugal.

Like Lopes, this man was about five foot six and compact, and wore a white singlet without any obvious insignia. Lopes had finished second to Virén in the 10,000-meter final five days earlier and was also entered in the marathon, although he had never run one before. Shorter had seen Lopes only briefly on the track, which explains his confusion about the identity of the man who ran next to him for the next six miles, matching him surge for surge, sprint for sprint. That man was Waldemar Cierpinski.

Cierpinski was not well-known, but he had run a 2:12:22 in the East German Olympic trials and was his country's top prospect. A former steeplechaser, he had been inspired to move up in distance following Shorter's victory at Munich. Indeed, he would later say what a wonderful feeling it was to come alongside the American and look "right into the eyes of the man who was my idol as a marathon runner. I knew all about him. And yet I could tell by the return glance that he didn't know much, if anything, about me."

Could Shorter have won if he had known his competitor was an experienced marathoner with fresh legs rather than the novice who had just won the silver medal on the track? Certainly, Shorter was not holding anything back. He threw in repeated bursts of speed, and each time he drew ahead of Cierpinski only to have the East German catch up again. Maybe if he'd known he was racing a marathoner rather than a track runner, he would have tried to break him earlier. And yet he was running as aggressively as possible, pushing the pace at every turn. True, he was hampered by the rain and the tightness in his legs, but he was also racing a man with what would turn out to be an unfair advantage.

When Cierpinski made his move, Shorter could not respond. At twenty miles, coming down a slight incline, the East German suddenly opened up a thirty-yard lead. Gradually, he increased it to one hundred yards. With three miles to go, Shorter tried to come back on him, gaining maybe half the ground, but Cierpinski took off again, and Shorter could not respond. Cierpinski entered the stadium with a fifty-second lead. Thinking there was still another four hundred meters to go, he circled the track while Shorter crossed the finish line and waited for him. Cierpinski's time was 2:09:55, a new Olympic record. Shorter came in second, in 2:10:46. Bill Rodgers limped home in 2:25:15.

The marathon concluded the Olympics, which was also notable for Bruce Jenner's victory in the decathlon, Alberto Juantorena's double victories in the 400 and 800 meters, and Nadia Comaneci's three gold medals. Five American boxers — Sugar Ray Leonard, Michael and Leon Spinks, Leo Randolph, and Howard Davis Jr. — won gold, and all except Davis went on to become professional world champions. Yet the games turned out to be a financial disaster for Montreal and put the city in debt for decades. They were boycotted by African nations to protest the New Zealand national rugby team's tour of South Africa. The Soviet Union and East Germany finished one-two in the medal count, yet their achievements were marred by accusations of drug use. When the American swimmer Shirley Babashoff charged her rivals with using steroids, as evidenced by their big muscles and deep voices, an East German Olympic official responded, "They came to swim, not to sing."

Many years later, however, when the files of the East German secret police, the Stasi, were opened, they would reveal State Plan 14:25, the country's drug program for its Olympic athletes. During the time of the plan, East German women swimmers broke 130 world records and won more than half of all the Olympic medals for which they were eligible. East Germany became an Olympic power-house, always at the top of the medal count. And there in the plan, on page 105, code number 62, was Waldemar Cierpinski.

Rudy Chapa and Alberto Salazar training at the University of Oregon.

Courtesy University of Oregon

From left: Bob Hodge, Vince Fleming, Randy Thomas,
Bill Rodgers, Frank Shorter, Tom Derderian, and George Reed
hit the beach at the 1976 Falmouth Road Race.

Courtesy Charlie Rodgers

10

Three for the Road (1976)

At a track meet, there would be your parents and twenty-two
other people. At a road race, you were a rock star.
— MIKE ROCHE

ALBERTO SALAZAR STOOD with his father and brother
on Washington Street in Wellesley, Massachusetts. From
where they waited, they could hear the "scream tunnel," rows of young women from Wellesley College who crowded
the road and screamed encouragement to the runners in the 1975
Boston Marathon. Wellesley was the halfway mark of the 26.2-mile
course, and the Wellesley women prided themselves on offering
raucous encouragement to all who passed by.

The lead police motorcycles and press truck came rumbling down
the road, and directly behind them was a skinny, sandy-haired guy
whom Alberto instantly recognized. It was like viewing the Academy
Awards and seeing your next-door neighbor stepping onto the stage
to collect his gold statue. "I know that guy!" Alberto blurted out. "I
run with him!" The three Salazars watched Bill Rodgers sail past, his
hand-lettered G B T C T-shirt validating the club with which José had

permitted his son to spend Tuesday evenings. Maybe they weren't Communists after all.

If Rodgers's victory at Boston heralded a new chapter in the running boom, the moment also was exhilarating and electrifying for the young Salazar, and it would have a profound effect on him. He was only sixteen years old, but suddenly he saw the future, and it was the marathon. If Rodgers could do it, Salazar thought, so could he. He knew that he kept pace with the older man in the GBTC workouts, and he was faster than Rodgers had been at the same age. If he kept working, he believed, there was nothing that could keep him from surpassing Rodgers's records and becoming the greatest distance runner the United States had ever known.

Pretty heady thoughts for a teenager, and probably a good thing he kept them (mostly) to himself. As it was, he still couldn't get a date or a second glance from the popular crowd at school. His confidence on the track did not translate into the real world, and he spent most of his senior year hiding behind his glower and his workouts. He was a dork, and he knew it, but he was also fast. Running was a convenient excuse for missing the parties, the prom, and his high school graduation, and he pretended not to mind that he'd never had a girlfriend.

It didn't help that he was often sick. His lifelong battle with illness and injury began at an early age. Although he later attributed his recurring bronchial infections and strep throats to an undiagnosed case of exercise-induced asthma, intense physical effort can also compromise the immune system. A teenager, who needs more sleep than an adult, whose immune system is still developing, and who is routinely exposed to viruses by classmates, is a walking petri dish. Although asthma can cause bronchitis, it is unlikely to cause strep. It's also unlikely to have gone dormant while Salazar was running some of his best races, then reappeared afterward. Indeed, in his memoir, *14 Minutes,* Salazar tells the story of how he snuck out of bed one time while suffering from strep throat and went for an hourlong run in the snow. When he returned, icicles clung to his nose, and he was shivering uncontrollably. Small wonder he suffered frequent infections.

Alberto punished his body like someone who had something to atone for. Although he rebelled against his father's strict Catholicism, it manifested itself on the roads. In terms of sheer mileage, he never ran farther than Shorter or Rodgers, despite later reporting that he logged more than two hundred miles a week. He might not even have run harder. (It's debatable whether anything he did rivaled Shorter's sixteen quarter-miles at altitude.) But he did his workouts at an earlier age, when his body was not prepared for it, and this would have a devastating effect on his future.

For some people, pain is a signal to stop. For Alberto Salazar, it was a signal that he was doing something right. Each pain threshold he crossed convinced him that he was tougher and stronger than anyone around him. Each injury or illness was a challenge to overcome. Running was his form of sadomasochism; he took pleasure in the abuse. He might be ungainly and unpopular, without Ricardo's grace or his father's charisma, but on the roads he was immortal, a demigod in a singlet and racing flats.

The colleges came calling. Running was not football, but among a certain set he was worth his weight soaking wet. Programs such as those at Villanova and Wisconsin had a long tradition of distance running, and there skinny was an asset, not a liability. His father wanted him to go to Harvard and become a doctor — the immigrant's dream. Running wouldn't pay the bills, he told Alberto, and it wouldn't help him survive a shooting war against the Communists. But Alberto had different ideas. Running was his future, the only plan he ever had, and he never seriously considered doing anything else. His classmates were going to Tufts, Bowdoin, Williams, Brown — good New England schools with solid academic credentials. Alberto wanted none of that. There were only two colleges he considered, and not because of their academic programs: Stanford and Oregon.

Stanford, a wealthy private university in the foothills of Palo

Alto, California, had a rich history of producing Olympians and national champions. Its beautiful mission-style architecture and perfect weather made it as easy for Alberto to love as a leggy blonde. The University of Oregon, a public university without Stanford's resources and set amid the gloom of rainy Eugene, had at best a mediocre academic reputation. It attracted mostly West Coast students who couldn't get in to the better public universities in California and Washington. Stanford was the "Harvard of the West," while Oregon was more like SUNY Binghamton without the snow.

But what Oregon had—in part because it lacked Stanford's largesse—was an incomparable running program at the center of the university. Oregon was the home of Bill Bowerman and Steve Prefontaine, running legends who gave the campus something to boast about. Oregon couldn't compete with Stanford's engineering department or basketball team or medical school, and so it didn't. It bestowed its attention on track and field and cheered its sons like returning war heroes. Stanford's stadium held 80,000 people, while the stadium at Hayward Field held about 11,000. But Hayward rocked at every track meet, filled to the rafters with fans who knew a good distance medley when they saw one. It was sacred ground, haunted by ghosts, an inspiration to anyone who stepped up to the line. In Salazar's mind, Hayward Field was the Fenway Park of track and field.

Coach Bill Dellinger, Bowerman's protégé, flew out to Boston to meet the Salazar family. José Salazar made him watch Alberto's running videos late into the night, which deeply embarrassed the boy and convinced Dellinger to cut back on his traveling in the future. But he did make one other trip that spring—to Indiana to visit the family of Rudy Chapa. Chapa was one of the most heralded high school runners the United States has ever produced. He held the national high school records in the two-mile, which stood for thirty-seven years, and the 10,000 meters, which still stands. As a schoolboy, he ran a 4:04 mile and eventually broke four minutes in the race. (Dellinger considered Chapa the second-best runner he ever coached. Prefontaine was first.) Like Salazar, Chapa was enamored with the mystique of Oregon, and the two boys talked by phone late into the night about their choices. Chapa was set on Oregon from the beginning, and it took little convincing to bring his new friend Alberto around.

Salazar was itching to get out of Wayland and his father's home. He chafed under the older man's temper and volatility, and they fought frequently. College couldn't arrive quickly enough, or be far enough away, and he counted down the days to his freedom. He missed his senior prom to run in a regional track championship and then skipped his high school graduation to attend the junior national track championships. Running was all that mattered, the only place where he could truly express himself and feel at ease.

The week before he was set to leave, his GBTC teammates convinced him to drive down to Cape Cod to run a road race. The race was the baby of the bartender at the Eliot Lounge, a man Salazar had met when the team deigned to invite him out for beers. Everyone was going, even Bill Rodgers, who was back from his demoralizing finish at the Montreal Olympics and itching for another crack at Shorter on the roads. To Salazar, it felt like a farewell party for a life to which he might not return, and he gladly agreed to join in.

More than two thousand people had registered for the fourth running of the Falmouth Road Race, and another five hundred would run unofficially. Thirty-five thousand spectators crowded the roads to watch. Every hotel room in town was occupied, and the restaurants and bars did a brisk business through the weekend. Except for the Boston Marathon, there were more people in Falmouth than Salazar had ever seen at any other single event.

Although Alberto did not understand the significance at the time, the 1976 Falmouth Road Race was the first time he would face Frank Shorter on the roads, and the first time Salazar, Shorter, and Rodgers would run against one another. To Shorter, Salazar was just a kid he barely remembered. To Rodgers, Alberto still had several years to train before he'd be ready for the big time. But the eighteen-year-old was not intimidated. He knew he was facing the two best distance runners in the world, but at this shorter distance, he felt he could be competitive. Both men had just run the Olympic marathon two weeks earlier, and their bodies might not have recovered. He planned to keep them both within range. If either faltered, anything could happen.

For the second time in four years, however, the weather cast a pall over the party. On Sunday morning, August 15, thundershowers threatened to turn the race into a wet slog. The downpour was more than just an inconvenience. While the elite athletes could stay dry in their coaches' vans and support vehicles, the rest of the field would have to endure waterlogged shoes, wet clothing, and a rainy chill while they waited for the race to begin. The roads would be slippery, and the finish line would be an unhappy mess for the hundreds of volunteers who would have to stand in the rain for several hours.

Fortunately, the showers ended well before the noon start, and the sun even peaked through the overcast sky. By the time the runners gathered on the aptly named Water Street in Woods Hole, most of the evidence of the deluge had evaporated, leaving only a few puddles and wet sidewalks.

Salazar joined his teammates at the starting line and said a quick hello to Rodgers, then introduced himself to Shorter. The latter was mobbed with admirers. Shorter was the most famous distance runner in the world, a two-time Olympic medalist, and in this crowd he drew everyone's eye. Rodgers was the U.S. record holder in the marathon and a favorite among the locals, but the smart money was still on Shorter.

With the clock counting down to noon, race organizers struggled to get the runners behind the starting line. John Carroll stood on the steps of the old firehouse and bellowed instructions into a megaphone, while Rich Sherman herded stragglers back over the drawbridge. Trying to move a crowd of two thousand people backward, however, was difficult if not impossible. The men in front would take two steps back, but the people behind them wouldn't move.

Soon everyone was crushed together, sweat-slicked bodies pressed up against one another. "Move, people!" Sherman shouted, but it was like yelling at a hill.

There was no handbook for managing the logistics of a road race, and until that year no one had to handle so many runners. Suddenly, Falmouth became a case study in crowd control as its organizers were forced to scramble with traffic management, event planning, sanitation engineering. Local homeowners complained about runners urinating (and defecating) on their lawns, while the police department and chamber of commerce complained about traffic jams and ferry delays. Neither Sherman nor Carroll had any background in event planning, and along with their wives, Kathy and Lucia, they fumbled and invented solutions on the fly, arguing over details and arrangements, bickering like a long-married couple who stayed together for the children.

Finally, Shorter managed to squeeze his heels behind the painted line. Rodgers tucked in nearby, and Salazar stood just a few paces away. A ripple of energy passed through the crowd as the runners tensed for the starting gun. It was more than the anticipation of the race ahead; it was the electric current of possibility, the presence of greatness, the boundless optimism of the open road, the gauntlet about to be thrown down. Then the gun sounded, and the runners charged across the line.

Four thousand feet went over the drawbridge, the ones in the back slowing to a shuffle. But the leaders cleared the fray with ease; by the crest of the first hill, they were in a pack that had already separated itself from the sub-elite. Amby Burfoot, Rodgers's former roommate, was in the lead, followed closely by his GBTC teammate Bob Hodge, who moved out in front at the Nobska Lighthouse.

It was humid, and no one was really pushing the pace. Through two miles, the leaders were in a tight group. But as the runners passed the three-mile mark, Rodgers and Shorter began to move away from the competition without consciously intending it. They simply matched each other step for step, and each stride pulled them a few more inches ahead of their rivals. For the next mile, their lead lengthened as the road opened. Salazar settled into the second pack with Burfoot, Hodge, and several other GBTC runners, each hoping the two in front would duel each other into the ground and leave an opening through which he could slip.

Although the dark-haired Shorter, with his effortless, high-stepping, efficient stride, and the blond Rodgers, with his floppy, pigeon-toed one, could not have been more different, they fell into a strange sort of sync as they ran — each man respecting the other too much to draft behind him; neither confident enough to pull ahead. Their arms moved in rhythm; their feet struck the ground in time. Individually, they were like two racecars built on different platforms, powered by different engines, and sporting different tires, yet together they revved like a single machine.

But just before the four-mile mark, as he had done the previous year, Shorter took off, and Rodgers could not go with him. Shorter opened a lead that widened with every step as he raced past the marina and into Falmouth Heights. An unbroken line of spectators cheered him on, whistling and clapping and calling his name. By the time he ascended the final hill, he had two hundred yards on Rodgers and was on his way to his second consecutive victory. He crossed the finish line in a new course record of 33:13. Rodgers eased in twenty-three seconds later, faster than the previous year, but not fast enough.

In the second pack came a string of GBTC runners: Randy Thomas, George Reed, and then Alberto Salazar, running quick and strong, outkicking Amby Burfoot and Bob Hodge to finish fifth. It was his last race as a high schooler, his first against Frank Shorter, and the beginning of his battles with Bill Rodgers to become the king of the roads.

Bill Rodgers winning his first New York City Marathon in the inaugural five-borough version of the race.

Associated Press

11

New York, New York (1976)

It was like everybody in America started running on the same day.
—AMBY BURFOOT

THE BROTHERS FOUR WAS rocking with its usual assort-
ment of freaks, clowns, and long-distance runners. The beer
flowed freely, and the jukebox played a rocking tune from a
band named for the city from which it emerged. Like that city, the
band Boston was largely ignored until good luck, propitious timing,
and some soaring arrangements propelled it to the top of the charts.

For years, Boston was one of only two cities in the United States
that regularly hosted a marathon. (Yonkers was the other.) With its
large collegiate community, it churned out runners like other cities cranked out unemployment statistics. When the pedestrianism
craze waned, Boston kept the torch lit with team races, all-comers
track meets, and, of course, the footrace starting in Hopkinton on
the third Monday in April. Boston barely ranked in the urban hi-
erarchy, with a subway system that resembled a children's toy, but
among runners it was Shangri-la.

The boom began in places such as Boston and obscure backcountry towns that embraced the sport at an opportune moment. From Falmouth to Peachtree to Lynchburg to Bix, most of the major U.S. road races emerged in seemingly random places that had in common the singular vision of a local hero and the coming together of like-minded souls. Falmouth had little to offer in the way of resort amenities — no sandy beaches or warm ocean surf — and couldn't compete for tourists against its Lower Cape neighbors Wellfleet, Truro, and Provincetown. Yet Tommy Leonard's genius and the indefatigable efforts of John Carroll and Rich Sherman put it in the right place at just the right time.

When it came to running, the real estate rule of *location, location, location* was practically meaningless. Runners raced where the locals would have them, and if that meant enduring the heat, humidity, and grasshoppers of the Quad Cities in summer, so be it. In those early years, runners were a close-knit fraternity of the chapped-lipped and knobby-kneed, resigned to their status as second-class citizens and happy just to fill their lungs with fresh air and their muscles with glycogen — and not be hit by a bus.

But all that was about to change. Falmouth caught the wave as it began to swell. The man standing near the jukebox at the Brothers Four would catch it as it crested. As he drank and swayed to the music, he could feel the beat of a brand-new hit.

Fred Lebow was born Ephraim Fishl Lebowitz in Romania in 1932. He survived the Holocaust and in 1949 immigrated to New York, where he Americanized his name. Thin, hooknosed, and stoop-shouldered, he resembled a canny bird, maybe an osprey or a falcon. As a young man, he smuggled diamonds from Belgium to England, wrapping them in condoms and slipping them into his body. Later, he worked in New York City's Garment District, eventually opening his own shop where he produced knockoffs of designer products.

Lebow was an avid tennis player and took up running simply to improve his stamina. Soon, however, it became his passion and obsession. As George Hirsch, publisher of *New York* magazine and

Runner's World, wrote, Lebow was "a blend of high priest of our sport and P. T. Barnum promoter — a man on a mission." He had no hobbies and no other serious interests, was never married, and threw himself into running like a man in the throes of a desperate affair, disregarding reason and the warnings of more sober acquaintances. Once, on New Year's Eve, he realized he was nineteen miles short of his yearly goal of 2,500 miles. He was living with a woman at the time, and the couple had been invited to a formal dinner, but he headed out into the snow to spend several hours jogging in Central Park. When he returned, all his belongings were stacked in the hallway with a farewell note pinned to the top.

Lebow embodied the spirit of the age. He once told a reporter, "I feel running is the oasis in life, the one area unlike business or relationships where one does not cheat or exaggerate. I will never write in my log that I ran a mile more than I really did. Running is my area of total honesty." That he was slow and without talent did not dissuade him.

His first race was a five-miler that consisted of eleven laps around Yankee Stadium and in which he finished second to last. In his debut marathon, the Cherry Tree Marathon in the Bronx, he posted a time of 4:09. Despite the traffic, the tenements, and the kids throwing stones at the runners, he was hooked. He loved the inclusiveness of the sport, the way the Sunday schleppers could participate in the same event with the elite. His biographer, Ron Rubin, suggested that Lebow's "Jewishness" and a childhood spent in isolation drove him to want to bring people together. Running was his means to create the family he never had.

But Lebow could not understand why anyone would plan a social event in the shadow of Yankee Stadium on a cold February morning. The Cherry Tree Marathon was run up and down Sedgwick Avenue, chosen for its lack of cars and spectators, not its beauty. It was a drab, dreary, and lonely slog. There were no water stops; instead, the runners were offered bourbon as they circled the stadium.

Lebow believed that running shouldn't just be an activity for the fleet of foot and the faithful, the elites who jabbered on about their split times and training methods. Like Tommy Leonard, he wanted to share his passion with the masses. But unlike Tommy, he saw the elite athletes as a means to achieve that end. He was first and foremost a salesman, and if elitism meant he couldn't sell his product to the widest possible audience, he didn't want anything to do with it. Not surprisingly, this would prove to be a source of conflict between him and the athletes he was courting.

With inclusiveness as his goal, he urged the New York Road Runners club to move the Cherry Tree Marathon to Central Park, but the club turned down his request, in part because the park was deemed too unsafe to draw runners. Undeterred, he took his proposal directly to the city's parks department. He promised the assistance of anonymous millionaires who, he claimed, supported the race and would bear its cost. To his surprise, the parks department bought his lie and approved the race. Thus the New York City Marathon was born.

The inaugural race, held on September 13, 1970, was not a resounding success. The temperature was 80 degrees at the start, and according to *Sports Illustrated,* there were more pushcart salesmen than spectators. As runners passed, the salesmen yelled, "What's the big rush? Stop and buy a pretzel already." One hundred twenty-seven people, including two women, paid one dollar to enter, but only fifty-five finished. New York firefighter Gary Muhrcke, who had worked a full shift the night before, won in 2:31:39.

By 1975, the race had grown to 534 entrants. Although Central Park was a better location than the busted roads of the Bronx, it was still a boring, repetitive circling of the same loop, with runners fighting cyclists, pedestrians, dogs, horseback riders, and drug dealers for turf.

There things might have stood — runners fighting for traction in the park while the life of the city pulsed around them — had George Spitz, a city auditor and runner, not proposed that the race traverse all five boroughs in honor of the nation's bicentennial. At first, the idea of shutting down city streets for an amateur athletic competition gave Lebow conniptions. He thought the cost of a five-borough marathon would be prohibitive and the logistics daunting. To say nothing of the personal dangers. A killer named "Son of Sam" was on the loose, and the streets were not safe for children and other living things. Times Square was not the Disney playground it is today, but the seedy home of prostitutes and thugs. Residents carried extra cash in their wallets so that muggers would not shoot or knife them. As the *New York Daily News* columnist Jim Dwyer wrote, "City Hall was bankrupt. Business was fleeing. The Bronx was burning. The popular wisdom was that most people wanted to run away from New York, not around it."

Spitz, however, was undaunted. He approached Manhattan borough president Percy Sutton, who had been a supporter of the 1975 marathon and who immediately cozied up to the idea of a five-borough course that would celebrate the city's ethnic diversity. Sutton promised he would help find funding, and he approached Mayor Abraham Beame for his approval. Beame had plenty of other things to worry about, so with Sutton's assurance that he would "take care of it," the mayor approved, because he "just thought it would be a nice thing for New York City."

Sutton secured a $25,000 sponsorship from real estate developers Jack and Lewis Rudin. With money and political backing, the implausible began to look a lot more plausible. In the face of building momentum, Lebow, always the pragmatist, wisely overcame his own objections. He lined up additional sponsorships from Manufacturers Hanover and Finnair, and he worked with Sutton and members of the New York Road Runners (of which he was now president) to outline the course.

Suddenly, Lebow had a race on his hands. But now, after expending his political capital, he had to make it pay off. Lebow may have had the heart of an idealist, but he had the brain of a salesman and micromanager. He knew that in order to have a big race, he needed to recruit big names. And the two biggest names in U.S. distance running were Frank Shorter and Bill Rodgers.

With that in mind, he traveled to Falmouth in August 1976. That was what he was doing in the Brothers Four, nursing a beer and trying to make himself heard over the jukebox. Falmouth had already achieved what Lebow dreamed about for New York: the crowds, the spirit, the beer. The New York City Marathon was nothing compared to the street party that was the Falmouth Road Race. A mere quarter of its size, with a less competitive field, New York was an afterthought on the running circuit. But Lebow aimed to change that, with the help of Falmouth's first- and second-place finishers.

Lebow congratulated Shorter and put an arm around Rodgers. To his detractors, he was irascible and short-tempered, but he also could be charming when the situation called for it. He was everyone's favorite uncle, the kind you love even after realizing he's stolen your wristwatch. Now he poured it on as he described the revamped New York City Marathon to Shorter and Rodgers. The race would begin in Staten Island, then continue over the Verrazano Bridge, through the boroughs of Brooklyn and Queens, into Manhattan via the Queensboro Bridge, and up to the Bronx, before ending in Central Park.

In truth, the marathon was an easy sell. Rodgers had run New York previously and was always up for another race. Shorter wanted to see how the city would handle shutting down the streets so that runners could pass. Both men liked the timing of a race in mid-September. They shook hands, and the deal was done.

But after agreeing to run, Rodgers insisted on a $2,000 appearance fee. Lebow claimed to be outraged; paying Shorter's travel expenses was one thing, but paying someone a fee simply to show up was scandalous. ("Does he think I'm going to take the money and not run?" Rodgers asked, rhetorically, later.) Never mind that the event was bringing the New York Road Runners thousands of dollars, or that without Rodgers (and Shorter) the race would be no better than a communal jog through the five boroughs. Lebow expected the athletes to donate their time in service to the greater good. Whether this was sheer opportunism or unabashed idealism — or a little of both — it reflected the inherent conflict between race organizers and elite runners. The former were usually noncompetitive hoofers who saw running as a form of mass expression, while the latter felt their hard work and dedication made them no different from other professional athletes who were richly remunerated. In any event, Lebow caved, and on the day before the marathon, he sent a courier with $2,000 in cash to Rodgers's hotel room.

Now Lebow had his race. With Shorter and Rodgers as a draw, and the unique lure of traversing New York City on foot, applications quadrupled. Suddenly, a small event in a dirty park became a citywide festival with some of the best distance runners in the world. Lebow also managed to recruit Ron Hill and Ian Thompson from Great Britain, as well as Akio Usami from Japan and Pekka Päivärinta from Finland, all top runners and each capable of winning. The race was billed as the "NYC Bicentennial Five-Borough Marathon," and whatever happened, the organizers were assured of making history, if not necessarily stopping traffic.

At 10:30 a.m. on October 24, 1976, the runners gathered at the Staten Island end of the Verrazano Bridge. It was a clear, crisp day, with temperatures perfect for running. To the runners looking out over the water, with the Wall Street skyline in the distance, it seemed an impossible vision. They were about to embark on a twenty-six-mile adventure, using the oldest means of transportation to travel paths designed for the newest. A giddy sense of anticipation swept the crowd. The city was laid out before them — both literally and figuratively — and for one day it felt as if they ruled.

Neither Rodgers nor Shorter, however, paid much attention to the view. When Percy Sutton fired the starter's pistol, they were thinking only of the miles ahead. They let Päivärinta take an early lead, running a 4:45 pace through the first five miles. At eight miles, he was forty-two seconds in front. But Shorter was not impressed. He had raced Päivärinta before, in Fukuoka. "He died there, and he died today," Shorter said later. Sure enough, at the ten-mile mark, Rodgers caught him, as did the Brit Chris Stewart. They eased up for a moment and then went past him. By the time they reached the Queensboro Bridge, Päivärinta was far behind.

But so, too, was Shorter. He had been feeling pain in his left foot and was favoring his right, which made his stride awkward and uncomfortable. By thirteen miles, he knew he couldn't catch Rodgers. He could see his rival up ahead, running easily, but all he could do was struggle to maintain his form. He felt the connection slipping, and suddenly it was a two-man race.

The runners came off the bridge and down onto FDR Drive. This meant navigating two flights of steps. Rodgers could not believe that a road race would include stairs. Not only did they slow his pace, but they were also dangerous. The organizers had been unable to shut down sixty blocks in midtown Manhattan, however, so the steps were a compromise, bringing the runners onto the roadway, where one lane was closed to traffic. The East River was gray and dead-looking, but at least there was a breeze, which diffused the pollution from the morning traffic.

Despite his concerns, Rodgers had no trouble on the stairs, and no real competition on the roads after that. He pushed the pace and left Stewart behind as he cruised into the Bronx. Then he made a U-turn and headed back into Manhattan over the Willis Avenue Bridge. In Central Park, he had to dodge race vehicles and police vans that simply stopped in front of him and parked. The finish line was pure chaos, with crowds pushing in on both sides. Family, friends, adoring fans, and tourists caught up in the unexpected crush awaited the runners. Rodgers accelerated up the final hill by Tavern on the Green and crossed the line in 2:10:10.

It was, he wrote later, "the easiest marathon for a fast time that I've ever run." More important, he beat Shorter by three minutes — his first victory over his rival in a marathon. Although he played down the significance of that fact, he knew the public viewed him as the second-best distance runner in the United States. Even he had begun to doubt his ability to beat Shorter when it mattered. After that day, however, his self-assurance grew, and he understood that the difference between victory and defeat was sometimes just a state of mind. He hadn't completely exorcised the demons of Montreal, and the absence of an Olympic medal would continue to haunt him, but the psychological barrier he had erected fell away. It was as if he'd injected himself with a dose of confidence that would carry him into the second half of the decade and to the top of the running pyramid.

The 1976 New York City Marathon was also a huge success for the city and the sport. What organizers envisioned as a one-shot deal turned into a repeat performance. Since its inception, it has drawn more than a million runners, with as many as 45,000 competing at one time, and has brought billions of dollars in revenue to New York. It also revolutionized the way road races were marketed and sold. It smashed the mystique of the marathon as an event for fanatics and accomplished Lebow's goal of inclusiveness. Despite its relatively recent origin, it became the model for hundreds of other big-city marathons.

In its success, however, lay the seeds of failure. With his emphasis on expanding the reach of his beloved activity and bringing it to the masses, Lebow undermined running as a sport. His focus on recruiting elite runners as a marketing tool diminished their value as athletes, while his stubborn refusal to pay them fairly for their efforts disrespected their achievements. As the event grew in size and revenue, the racing itself became an afterthought, with more attention paid to participating than winning. This disconnect — between finishing the race and racing the race — significantly affected the way people approached running and embraced the boom. Soon it would spell the sport's doom.

Bill Rodgers (#2) leading Frank Shorter (#1),
Alberto Salazar (#20), Hillary Tuwei (#41), and
Rudy Chapa (#21) at the 1977 Falmouth Road Race.

Associated Press

12

The Ligaments That Bind (1977)

We trained to the point where we could feel we were breaking
down. It resulted in Frank being the best marathoner in the world,
so I'd like to think we were doing something productive.

— JACK BACHELER

E VERY COMPETITIVE RUNNER has about ten good years in
his legs. Some, genetically blessed, have a few more. Others,
not as fortunate, have less. The biological and biochemical
explanations are complicated, but in essence it comes down to this:
elasticity. The youthful body stretches and conforms, accommodat-
ing overindulgence and trauma. During physical activity, muscles
are expanded and contracted like taffy — sometimes to the breaking point. Indeed, the process of muscle building *requires* muscle
destruction. As the body repairs the damage to cellular structures,
muscles grow bigger and stronger. But over time, elasticity suffers.

Frank Shorter heard the pop on February 14, 1976, during an interval workout on the indoor track at the University of Colorado.
It wasn't exactly the pop heard round the world, but it would reso-
nate through the sport of distance running, rippling outward from

Shorter's foot to the greater corpus of the running community. Perhaps if he had been two years younger the injury would have healed differently, or the scar tissue that eventually formed around his damaged ligament would have resolved without the need for surgery. But he was twenty-eight, with eight hard years of running in his legs, and no longer was the supple runner of his youth. The damage he had done while running his quarter-miles on the track made his hamstrings and quadriceps tighter and prone to tearing. The careful stretching he did was no longer sufficient to loosen them up completely. Like the musclebound outfielder who pulls up lame while sprinting to first base, his fitness was his weakness. It was only a matter of time.

Although scientists don't fully understand what causes cellular damage, it's clear that decreased cell function results in the deterioration of tissue and in the body's ability to perform at maximum levels. Some suggest that free radicals — molecules lacking a stable electron pair as a result of normal metabolic processes — damage other molecules in the cell by stealing their electrons and causing a chain reaction that eventually leads to cell death. Athletes, whose metabolism is constantly revving at a higher rate, may succumb more quickly to cellular damage than the average couch potato (although their stronger hearts and leaner physiques compensate for this decay). Genetic mutation may also play a role — the inevitable errors that occur when cells divide, causing degeneration, cell death, and "retirement" (when cells stop dividing).

Regardless of the mechanism, age, trauma, stress, and disease contribute to the deterioration of the human body over time. Muscle fibers shrink in diameter, which causes a loss of strength and endurance, and fast-twitch fibers degenerate more quickly. (If they're not exercised enough, they may never come back.) As muscle mass decreases, it is replaced with fat, water, and other tissue. Over time and too many miles, fibrous tissue builds up, decreasing flexibility and range of motion. As flexibility decreases, the stride is shortened, which in turn leads to further risk of injury. In addition, as humans

142

age, osteoclasts, which break down bone, begin to outnumber os-
teoblasts, which build it up. This leads to a decrease in bone density
and strength. Although weight-bearing exercise such as running
slows the breakdown, it can't stop the process. As a result, older
runners are more prone to stress fractures and other injuries of the
lower extremities, which bear most of the stress from a runner's
miles on the roads.

But it's not just the constant pounding that leads to a diminish-
ment in athletic performance. The body needs oxygen for fuel, and
the two systems designed to provide it — respiratory and circula-
tory — eventually lose their ability to keep up with the demands
of the elite runner. Like other tissue, the lungs lose their elasticity,
which diminishes their capacity to process oxygen efficiently. The
diaphragm — a muscle that expands the chest so that we can in-
hale — gets weaker, reducing the amount of air that makes it into
the lungs. Even without this falloff, there isn't enough room for the
same volume of air, because the size of the thoracic cavity decreases
as a result of the thickening of the surrounding tissue. With less
oxygen processed less efficiently, the muscles of the legs and arms
are already at a disadvantage before the first sprint.

Meanwhile, the delivery system — the heart and blood vessels — is
compromised as runners age. Although running strengthens the
heart and can widen blood vessels, there is some evidence that extreme training can actually damage the heart, causing a buildup of
fibrous tissue that increases the risk of heart attack. In addition, no
amount of strengthening can prevent the decline in the elasticity of
cardiac tissue or the loss of receptors that connect cardiac tissue to
the central nervous system. These processes lead to a slower heart-
beat and lower the pumping capacity of the heart. With time, fat
and plaque build up along the artery walls, making them stiffer and
the passages narrower. All of this diminishes blood flow and oxygen
delivery to the muscles.

Once oxygen gets to the muscles, the maximum amount the
body can metabolize, or VO_2 max, decreases, perhaps as a result of

damage to the mitochondrial cells. Although exercise can slow this decline, it begins inexorably around age twenty-five. Thus, while it might have seemed to Shorter, Rodgers, and Salazar that they were getting faster and stronger, the processes leading to their decline were already in place. They couldn't avoid it; they could only hope to stave off the inevitable and pray their good years would last longer than most.

For Frank Shorter, the day of reckoning had already arrived. He had suffered minor injuries in the past, but these always healed, and he continued to run as fast as before, if not faster. Now he felt the pain on the inner part of his foot, in an area he would later identify as the talonavicular joint, the lowest of three joints that make up the ankle. The ligaments that hold the bones together had degenerated, and eventually "bone spurs" formed. These were not actually spurs, but new bone that rubbed against the soft tissue and made running more painful.

He was at a loss to explain the source of the injury. He hadn't fallen or twisted his ankle. No one had spiked him or dropped a weight on his toe. Like most running injuries, it began in the lower back and hamstrings, then migrated down to the calves. The muscles tightened from stress and overuse, which put more pressure on the tendons, which pulled on the bones, which stretched the ligaments so they were like guitar strings waiting to be plucked. The slightest pressure from the normal force of running would snap them.

In that respect, Shorter's injury, although it occurred in a less common area of the foot, was quite normal. As with most significant running injuries — plantar fasciitis, Achilles tendonitis, iliotibial band syndrome, shin splints, and even stress fractures — overtaxed and fatigued muscles put pressure on the surrounding tissue, until something gives. Because muscles are generally bigger, heavier, and denser, they usually win. (Muscle tears are unusual in distance runners, though more common among sprinters.) The secret to avoiding injuries (besides not getting old) is to give muscles sufficient time to acclimate and recover.

But the elite runner is always on the knife-edge of injury and fitness. Too much pounding, and he's incapacitated; too little, and he loses. Even after experiencing the pop, Shorter continued to train and race. He believed he could "run through it," and, in fact, the pain subsided for a time. Partly, his body was able to repair and mask the injury. Partly, pain is just a natural part of road racing, and he was simply inured to running through it. Distance-running injuries are rarely immediately incapacitating like a torn Achilles tendon or a compound fracture. Instead, they creep up on a runner, then punch him in the gut.

The foot was sensitive enough for Shorter to pass up trying to double in the 10,000 meters and the marathon at the Montreal Olympics. It flared up again at the New York City Marathon in the fall. Yet a few months later, he won the AAU 10,000-meter championship. Then, over the Fourth of July weekend, he won the inaugural Chicago Distance Classic, a twenty-kilometer road race, and, on the very next day, the Peachtree Road Race in Atlanta, a ten-kilometer race that rivaled Falmouth in size and prestige. At Peachtree, he beat both Bill Rodgers and Lasse Virén, pulling away from Rodgers with about half a mile to go. By August, it appeared he was prepped for his third straight victory at Falmouth. Who could touch him? Not the young Alberto Salazar, still not ready for prime time. Not Bill Rodgers, who Shorter believed "at the end of a race, in a one-on-one duel, would crack first."

Bill Rodgers was the same chronological age as Frank Shorter, and yet his legs were younger. The time spent loafing in college and smoking cigarettes in Boston turned out to be an advantage later on the roads. As Shorter struggled with his foot injury, Rodgers hit his stride. After winning the New York City Marathon, he notched victories at marathons in Sado Island and Kyoto, Japan, as well as in Baltimore, and he won a handful of road races and the two-mile at the Millrose Games — all in the span of four months. But in the spring of 1977, he was unable to complete the Boston Marathon on a hot (80-degree) day. As the defending champion and course record holder, it was a huge disappointment, but the strain of all the racing took its toll as he topped Heartbreak Hill, and he dropped out at the same point where he'd quit in 1973.

Rodgers was blessed with good genes. Racing nearly every weekend, and competing in more than one or two marathons a year, should have knocked a couple of years off his longevity. Today, no coach would permit it. But Rodgers had little to lose. There was no big payday in racing and no agents to negotiate a match race with Frank Shorter. A free plane ticket and a hot meal were enough to get him traveling. In fact, if he was going to eat, he had to race — wherever and whenever he could. Later, he was criticized for overracing, but it was his constant presence on the roads that gave the boom the kick it needed.

So when Shorter beat him at Peachtree, he didn't retreat to his compound in the mountains to reformulate strategy with a team of nutritionists, trainers, and public relations consultants. Sure, it irritated him that Shorter could race twenty kilometers and then beat him the next day at Peachtree, but he attributed that to Shorter's superior track speed, not his fitness. To beat Shorter, he simply had to run faster. That meant more intervals with the GBTC on the hills and outdoor track, and more races.

In early August, he ran seven repeat miles at a 4:40 pace, with only about a sixty-second rest between them. Then, on August 9, he set four U.S. records on the track at Boston University in the fifteen kilometers, twenty kilometers, ten-mile, and one-hour run (covering 12 miles, 1,351 yards, 2 feet). On Friday, August 19, as he drove down to Falmouth with Ellen, whom he'd married in 1975, he felt as if he was in the best shape of his life. He was healthy, the weather was decent, and he did not fear Shorter. He had heard his rival was nursing a foot injury, but he didn't believe it. Runners were hypochondriacs — always complaining about this little ache or that pain — and he had seen the man race at Peachtree.

The prerace "expo" was held at the Falmouth Recreation Center.

Shoe and clothing vendors hawked their wares alongside local banks offering free calendars and key chains. For the first time, the race had other legitimate contenders — Olympian Mike Roche, Kenyan Hillary Tuwei, Penn State standout Greg Fredericks, and Oregon teammates Alberto Salazar and Rudy Chapa — but the media still treated the event as a two-man race, and all the questions were about whether Shorter would win his third in a row.

There were now more than 2,800 entrants, the largest field to date. Tommy Leonard was running, but Rich Sherman and John Carroll drove the course in Carroll's Porsche, stopping long enough to take photos of the leaders, then hopping back in the car and zooming ahead. According to the *Falmouth Enterprise,* they "acted like boys winning a game they had tried to win for a long time." Carroll was at the wheel, while Sherman sat on the door with a microphone in hand, radioing the positions of the leaders to a sound truck at the finish line. Sherman was not shy about his allegiances, as he shouted encouragement to Rodgers at every turn: "Go, Billy!" and "Get 'em, Bill!" Rodgers brought out that kind of devotion in his fans, and as the underdog, he had just about everyone's heart. To the Cape Cod crowd, he was the Boston Red Sox, while Frank Shorter, the gold and silver medalist from Colorado, was the Yankees.

Rodgers pushed the pace from the start. Conditions were perfect for him: moderate temperatures and low humidity. He took an early lead, shared it with Greg Fredericks momentarily as the runners hit Nobska Beach, and then regained it as they came around the lighthouse. Twice before, he had lost the race to Shorter by not going out hard enough, and he wasn't going to make that mistake again.

Shorter let him go. He was confident in his ability to outkick Rodgers, and he knew that he had seven miles to run. But something didn't feel right. Those first few steps were not as quick or easy, and his breathing felt labored. If he was going to win this race, he would need to loosen up and find his stride. So he tried to relax and let Rodgers set the pace. But in the back of his mind, the doubts had already crept in.

Alberto Salazar had no doubts. He wasn't going to lead the race, but he wasn't going to let Rodgers get too far out of his sight. The older runner was not his master, and he believed he had the better leg speed. He was surprised to find himself in front of Shorter this early in the race, but he didn't linger on it. Instead, he ran with Chapa to his right and Roche to his left and kept Rodgers within a couple of strides. The course was familiar, and the crowds felt like home. He let the momentum take him as he girded for the battle ahead.

By F. R. Lillie Road, Rodgers had opened a fifteen-yard lead. Salazar was next, running alone in an isolated pocket, followed quickly by Shorter, Roche, Tuwei, Fredericks, and Chapa in a second pack about two strides behind. They hit the three-mile mark with Rodgers in control, his lead lengthening by another five yards.

Meanwhile, the road had become crowded with cyclists, who tucked in behind Rodgers for a better view of the race. At one point, there were about twenty-five of them, all shapes and sizes, riding along as if on a Sunday spin around the park. Photographers in the press truck yelled at them to get off the road — they were blocking the view (and, by the way, obstructing the runners) — but it would take police a couple more miles to figure out something was wrong.

Fredericks made another move to grab back the lead, which gave Rodgers the push he needed to break open the race. With the runners strung out along Surf Drive, Rodgers took off and dropped Fredericks right there in his tracks. It was the same place Shorter had dusted him the previous two years, and Rodgers ran as if he were exorcising demons. He poured it on, his legs churning on the open road, his face contorting as he outdistanced his pursuers.

Shorter watched with a sense of frustration. He knew now for certain it wasn't his day. He had lost the thread and fell back behind Salazar, Fredericks, and Roche, then glanced behind him to see who was gaining. It was now a race to hold his place and save face on the great stage of Falmouth. There was losing, and then there was *losing*, and Shorter refocused on the former to avoid the latter.

Salazar was not thinking of losing. Not yet. Fredericks's battle with Rodgers had fatigued him, and Salazar picked him off like a wounded combatant. Then there was Rodgers, up ahead, and Salazar pushed himself to catch him: head down, knees lifting, his bottom-heavy gait surprisingly efficient. But he could not gain ground on Rodgers, seemingly unstoppable in the bright morning sun. Rodgers made the wide swing around the Falmouth marina, his lead increasing with every stride. The crowd spilled into the road, straining to catch a glimpse of the champion. Rodgers peeked over his right shoulder to see Salazar behind him, but unless Salazar had a 4:15 mile in him, he wasn't going to catch Rodgers.

Rodgers maintained his pace past the throngs gathered in front of the *Island Queen* ferry, through the intersection that led to the beach, and on to the final turn at the water, then he motored up the last hill. There was the finish line, one hundred yards downhill, and he waved to the crowd as he sprinted for the tape. He crossed the line in 32:23, smashing Shorter's course record by fifty seconds, and equalizing their road race standings at 7–7–1. Salazar came in second, in 32:40, followed by Fredericks, Roche, and then Shorter. And in a declaration that the boom was now gender neutral, 1976 Boston Marathon winner Kim Merritt shattered the women's course record by more than four minutes.

After the race, Rodgers drank a Perrier and answered reporters' questions. He expressed amazement at the new course record. He smiled broadly and said he'd had no expectations but was grateful that no one had challenged him after he made his last move.

Across the street from Rodgers stood the nineteen-year-old Salazar, his father's arm draped around him. When a local reporter asked how he felt, he responded, "It feels good to beat Frank Shorter." José Salazar beamed, proud of his son's achievement. He had beaten the Olympic champion and run the second-fastest time ever on the course. Rodgers called him a "sensation" and said he was "deadly." No one who had seen him run could disagree.

Although Shorter attributed his loss to his injured foot, the injury had not hampered him at Peachtree, and his time at Falmouth was just twenty seconds slower than his record the prior year. In September, he would run his best time ever in the 5000 meters. The truth was, on that course, on that date, no one was better than Bill Rodgers. Shorter believed, with the eternal optimism of the long-distance runner, that he would return. His foot would heal, his times would improve, and the ravages of age would never touch him. But he was wrong. The crown had been passed. There was a new king in town.

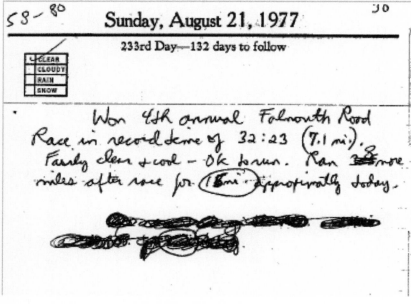

Bill Rodgers's training log.

Courtesy Bill Rodgers

13

Show Me the Money (1977)

After I set two world records, Fred Lebow asked me, "Didn't we pay
you anything?" I said, "No! I didn't even know there was money
available." I would have been happy just to eat, train, and race.

— GRETE WAITZ

THE RACE DIRECTORS came calling, bags of cash in hand.
They knew enough not to deal directly with the runners.
Instead, they paid off a coach, a spouse, a friend. It was an
open secret on the circuit that money talked, while runners hopped,
skipped, and sprinted to the bank. The convenient fiction that an
athlete could spend his days training and then engage in competition in which everyone profited but him was lunacy.

And yet lunacy prevailed. Like Rick's Café in *Casablanca*, Congress
pretended to be shocked — shocked! — when Frank Shorter testified
before the President's Commission on Olympic Sports that "we're all
professionals." His intention was to enlighten lawmakers about why
the United States was getting trounced in international competition.
He explained that the AAU controlled where and how athletes competed and forced them to live in poverty while providing no finan-

cial support. Meanwhile, other nations housed and fed their athletes and treated them like professionals. Yet Shorter's unfortunate utterance almost got him banned from international competition.

Shorter was right, however. The arbitrary distinction between amateurs and professionals was a relic from the British university system, and a means to keep the lumpenproletariat from competing with the upper classes. For years, so-called amateurs had evaded the rules by creative means, such as the 1928 Olympian with an open expense account at Brooks Brothers into which track promoters deposited his winnings. Henry Carr, the Olympic 200-meter champion in 1964, described payments "like in the James Bond or mystery movies . . . A shoe agent goes into the bathroom and leaves an envelope under the stall, and I go into the stall after him. You get an envelope that had six, seven hundred or a couple of thousand dollars." In 1968, a *Sports Illustrated* cover story reported Adidas and Puma "falling all over each other . . . at the Mexico City Olympics, signing up top track and field athletes to wear their shoes." Athletes took advantage of the rivalry and negotiated for the highest possible prices, averaging around $1,000 but sometimes getting as much as $10,000. In 1971, Bob Hersh published an exposé in *Track & Field News* in which he detailed an indoor 600-meter runner who charged "one dollar per yard" and once stepped off the track at the 500-meter mark when the meet promoter was short $100.

Most runners were not as obvious. Shorter found cash stuffed in his shoes. Rodgers had his wife, Ellen, handle his negotiations. California meet promoter Al Franken acknowledged he paid appearance fees to managers of track clubs, who then distributed the cash to their runners. It was an organized charade that still left most athletes with bills to pay and second jobs to work. The GBTC runners, for example, would squeeze in a twelve-mile run late at night after working all day delivering mail or walking the beat. The same year Bill Rodgers set a new U.S. record at the Boston Marathon, he worked for $1.65 an hour cutting lawns for his landlord, while NFL quarterback Joe Namath signed a $2 million endorsement deal with Brut.

Not everyone was impoverished, but none of them were compensated like professionals. The best-paid runners were milers, who often received more than $1,000 per race. In 1979, the American miler Steve Scott was ranked third in the world, and he earned $1,000 per race on the European track circuit, $10,000 per year for wearing a Sub-Four singlet, and another $10,000 per year for racing in New Balance sneakers. World champion high jumper Dwight Stones made an estimated $200,000 during the six-year period that he jumped as an amateur, from 1973 to 1979. He did this by double-booking meets on the same coast and pocketing half his transportation money. He also got performance bonuses: once he jumped a world-record height after holding out for a $500 bonus. He was pragmatic in his efforts to earn a living: he would get meet directors drunk, wouldn't accept certain foreign currencies, and engaged in "performance shaving." This meant he would do less than what he knew he was capable of at certain meets in order to guarantee further performance bonuses at future meets. Why break a record by an inch when he could break it by a half inch at one meet and another half inch at a second meet? Stones was eventually investigated by the IRS for these under-the-table payments, but he was kicked out of the AAU for "improperly allocating" money he'd won on a sports game show, not for any of the illegal payments he received during his career.

As running boomed, it became big business in the United States, with companies such as Puma, Adidas, and Nike raking in millions. Yet most of the athletes who made the companies rich were poor, subsisting, like Bill Rodgers, on food stamps or menial jobs. When Rodgers won the Boston Marathon, he was able to use his newfound fame to squeeze a few bucks out of race promoters, but he still kept his day job. Meanwhile, Frank Shorter started a line of running gear, but it took lengthy negotiations with the International Association of Athletics Federations (the world governing body for track and field), along with an agreement that he would own at least 51 percent of the business and not license his name, before he was permitted to do so. At that time, runners were prohibited from getting paid for giving clinics, endorsing products or equipment, or profiting from their fame in any way. In effect, they were barred from earning a living.

Rodgers called the system "shamateurism." Like Shorter, he was forced to own at least 51 percent of his running stores, which made it difficult to franchise them, and he was forbidden by amateur rules from using his photograph or his accomplishments to sell his running clothes. In 1979, he earned a mere $7,000 from his business and supplemented this income by accepting invitations to races in which directors gave him meal money, then took him to dinner anyway. He complained that the AAU took money from corporations for advertising at road races but gave nothing back to the runners. Rodgers argued that without prize money for athletes, the amateur system would not draw press coverage and, as a result, would never interest enough talented athletes for the United States to compete internationally.

History, however, would not prove him correct. When prize money was finally offered in road races, it served only to draw the East Africans out of their continent, and they proceeded to trounce the competition. By then, the top Americans — all of whom had competed without money — had faded from the scene. Money was not the magic pill that would bring gold medals in the distance events. Shorter won his without a dime, and no American has won one since. The lack of money, in fact, made it possible to run without strictures, to focus on the sport itself without the distractions of business. Shorter, Rodgers, and Salazar all ran at a time when the hunger for achievement coexisted with real hunger. The two complemented each other, perhaps more than money ever could.

Yet the story is also not that simple. Today the $50,000 offered for winning an elite marathon is about the same as a top baseball player makes each time he comes to bat. For an African kid raised on the veld, with running in his genes and his culture, the sum is enough to get him dreaming. For a talented American kid, it's peanuts. Thus we still live in a society in which running is the default sport for kids who can't play football, baseball, or basketball (or, increasingly, soccer or lacrosse) and the few fanatics who, through luck or good coaching, discover their muse. In a country increasingly obsessed with the almighty dollar, the latter group grows smaller and smaller.

When Tommy Leonard first brought Bill Rodgers and Marty Liquori to the Cape, he lured them with promises of free beer and bikini-clad women. To lodge them, he turned to his friends and neighbors, who offered their guest rooms. To feed them, volunteers cooked a spaghetti dinner at the high school gym. It was all very charming, but a far cry from the luxury hotels in which the Japanese housed Shorter and Rodgers when they ran Fukuoka. Overseas, it seemed, the same rules didn't apply. European track promoters openly distributed cash at track meets, while countries such as Finland and Czechoslovakia provided their runners with ersatz military jobs in order to give them time and money to train. In comparison, the U.S. running circuit was like a poor, unwashed cousin.

By 1977, a free spaghetti dinner and a guest bed were not enough to lure the top runners to Cape Cod. Falmouth needed money to compete against the Peachtree Road Race and other big races that were slipping cash into runners' shoes, drawing crowds, and making names for themselves. It needed more money than local businessman Bill Crowley could afford. At Fred Lebow's urging, Tommy traveled to New York on the Eastern shuttle to meet with representatives of the French mineral water company Perrier. He was dressed in his best blue blazer, which had one button missing, and a pair of khakis with a pizza stain. A woman with her hair pulled back in a blond bun ushered him into a conference room with stunning, unobstructed views of Central Park. There, men dressed in suits listened to him talk about the beauty of running past Nobska Lighthouse and along Surf Drive and heard his pitch for sponsoring the race.

He had them at "hello." Perrier's marketing strategy was tied to clean, healthy living, which dovetailed perfectly with the running boom. (It was already a sponsor of the New York City Marathon.) The Perrier executives found Tommy garrulous and charming, albeit poorly groomed. They quickly wrote him a check for $5,000 and considered it a steal. A print advertisement, they knew, would cost five times as much and reach fewer people. For a fraction of the price, the Falmouth Road Race gave them a summer-long publicity blitz, with the company's name mentioned in every news article about the race and plastered on T-shirts, banners, and posters throughout New England and beyond. It was a perfect "branding" opportunity, and Perrier soon became synonymous with running and fitness (although drinking fizzy water at the end of a race was the last thing many runners wanted to do).

What was more surprising was how little the major road races took advantage of these marketing opportunities. There was big money to be made in corporate sponsorships, and yet running never profited in the way that golf and other less compelling sports did. Today, it costs around $2 million to sponsor the New York City Marathon, one of the biggest running events in the world, while even the smallest PGA golf tournament rakes in at least that amount from its title sponsor, and the PGA Tour earns about $1 billion a year.

Of course, television helps. The millions of people who watch the Masters and other PGA events are manna from heaven to corporate sponsors. According to *SportsBusiness Daily,* the value of Nike's exposure during the final round of golf's four major tournaments in 2007 was $5.7 million. That same year, in the world of tennis, Lexus's sponsorship of the U.S. Open was worth about $12 million in advertising time on CBS. Thus companies are willing to shell out serious cash for the opportunity to participate in this advertising bonanza.

For the most part, running cannot count on television exposure. The New York City Marathon is broadcast locally, but not nationally. During its heyday, the Falmouth Road Race appeared on a fledgling cable channel, ESPN, but not live, and it was heavily edited. When running is televised, the announcers rarely know much about the sport and focus instead on human-interest stories rather than the race itself. Commercials interrupt the pacing, and it is not unusual for a key moment to happen offscreen and be ignored when the programming returns. TV executives seem to think running is just about putting one foot in front of the other, which doesn't make for dramatic television, even as they broadcast hours of soft-bellied men walking to retrieve a dimpled white ball as if it were the most exciting thing in the world.

Yet television ratings are also overrated. The people who measure these things assume that an athlete's T-shirt bearing a corporate logo counts as a free advertisement when viewed by the television audience. Then they calculate how much that commercial time would cost on the open market and write a check. But they discount, or ignore, the credibility an athlete brings to the brand simply by proclaiming his loyalty. Even without the television exposure, the fact that an athlete plays in Nike clothing or uses Adidas equipment makes a huge impression on the average fan. Television may get the word out, but only because millions of people might not otherwise know an athlete's preferences. On the roads, however, where millions of fans can see the sneakers, shorts, and T-shirts attached to bodies like human billboards, the power of television is muted. When Bill Rodgers won the Boston Marathon in a pair of Nikes, more than half a million people witnessed it firsthand, and millions more heard about it from friends in the running community. Nike is now the most valuable sports brand in the world. Yet it began as a running shoe company and sold its products not through television advertising, but through product placement on the feet of runners.

Money began to flow into the sport when the AAU and the IAAF relaxed their rules and allowed Shorter and Rodgers to start their businesses in 1977. In 1979, with the AAU's blessing, Shorter struck a deal with Hilton to become a paid consultant who helped promote the brand by offering guests running tips, healthy food choices, and training routes in cities where the hotels were located. But the big breakthrough occurred in 1981 when, after lobbying by Shorter, Rodgers, and others, the IAAF approved a "trust" system that permitted athletes to accept prize and appearance money as long as it was deposited into a trust fund and withdrawn only for "legitimate training expenses." After that, the floodgates opened, and eventually the arbitrary distinction between amateur and professional athletes collapsed.

Shorter, among others, bemoaned many of the changes he helped bring about. In 1984, he wrote, "Running seems to be taking on more of the characteristics of professional sport, and that may not be in its best interest." He pointed to the rise of agents as a factor in diminishing competition (because they pick and choose their clients' races and avoid many head-to-head matchups), and he foresaw a time when the best runners did not compete for the love of the sport, but the love of money.

That time would come sooner even than he predicted.

Mike Roche (#4) and Alberto Salazar (#2) lead the start
of the 1978 Falmouth Road Race.

Courtesy Falmouth Historical Society

14

Death's Door (1978)

*I remember sticking with Rodgers and telling myself I couldn't let
him get away. I don't remember anything after that.*
— ALBERTO SALAZAR

IN OREGON, ALBERTO SALAZAR unpacked his belongings
and set up camp with his roommate, Rudy Chapa. The two
young men cut romantic figures on a campus populated by pale
slackers from Northwest towns such as Gresham and Sutherlin.
With their olive skin, dark hair, and lean runners' physiques, they
were like Spanish gods among the heathen, and the women came
running. But if the coeds expected Bacchanalian revelry, they
were disappointed. Salazar was conservative and clean-cut, never
did drugs, drank sparingly, and went to sleep at a reasonable hour.
Chapa was more of a night owl, but he spent his time studying hard
rather than partying. His father was a day laborer, and although he
was as committed to running as Alberto, he knew an athletic career
had a short half-life and was already planning a future in finance or
law. For Alberto, there was only running.

Their coach, Bill Dellinger, was a three-time Olympian and the bronze medalist in the 5000 meters at the Tokyo Olympics in 1964. An Oregon graduate himself, Dellinger had been coached by Bill Bowerman, the cofounder of Nike. Dellinger became Bowerman's assistant, and when Bowerman retired in 1973, he took over. Although Dellinger modeled his training program after his mentor's, in temperament the two men were very different.

Bowerman was a fanatic — not just about equipment but also about training methods, nutrition, and fitness. His ninety-page book *Jogging,* written after visiting his friend and colleague Arthur Lydiard in New Zealand and originally published in 1966, sold one million copies and was widely credited with bringing Lydiard's coaching concepts to the United States and igniting interest in running. One of the greatest track coaches the United States ever produced, Bowerman directed the Oregon track-and-field program with a strong hand and a sharp mind. He was truly a visionary and not always the easiest person to be around. Dellinger, on the other hand, was more inclined to leave his charges to their own devices. He gave them the workout — usually a version of Bowerman's — and left them to accomplish it. If they cheated, it was not his job to police them.

Runners, however, always cheat. It's the nature of a sport in which individual achievement is just as important as, if not more important, than the success of a team. Unlike football, baseball, or basketball, runners can win when the team loses, and even a failing team can produce an NCAA or Olympic champion. Thus runners have a constant incentive to vary the training prescribed by their coaches, particularly when the coach tailors the training for the entire team. A superstar athlete — or an athlete who thinks he is a superstar — is likely to take the coach's instructions as a recommendation and modify them as he sees best.

Bowerman would never have permitted this. His battles with Steve Prefontaine over the runner's training were legendary. He knew what was best, and damn Prefontaine if the kid wouldn't listen. Bowerman would kick him off the track sooner than have him run an extra lap that wasn't prescribed.

Dellinger was more hands-off, however, and this led both Salazar and Chapa to take advantage. They were the two most highly touted prospects since Prefontaine, and they knew it. If Dellinger said eight intervals, they might do ten. If Dellinger said a 4:50 pace, they would drop down to 4:40. Salazar always had a problem holding back. From the moment he ran his first twenty-miler as a ninth grader, he pushed the limits of what other people said he couldn't do, whether it was his brother, his father, or Coach Squires. Now that he had a partner in crime, his lawlessness knew no bounds. Freed from the strictures of his father's home and Coach Squires's iron hand, there was little to restrain him. He ran as if the future could not arrive fast enough.

Indeed, it couldn't. His first year at Oregon was a disappointment. He got injured early and barely recovered in time to place ninth in the 5000 meters at the NCAA championships. This was respectable, but not what he expected of himself. He returned reluctantly to Wayland, where he spent the summer working construction for his father's company. Alberto and José would drive to New Hampshire together in the morning, and on the way home his father would drop him seven miles from the house so that he could run the rest of the way. It was exhausting, and he was always tired, but the year away had been good for him, and father and son settled into a sort of détente.

In August, his second-place finish at Falmouth was a huge lift. It proved to him that he had recovered from his injuries and his training was on pace. He was thrilled with his victory over Frank Shorter — almost as thrilled as his father. Back in Wayland, José shared the news with anyone who would listen: his son had beaten the Olympic gold medalist. It was a chest-thumping moment, and Alberto returned to Eugene with dreams of glory and Bill Rodgers on his mind.

That fall, the Oregon cross-country team, with sophomore Alberto Salazar among the top five, won the NCAA cross-country championships. More important, Alberto met his future wife, freshman Molly Morton, a Portland native who was also a distance runner. Molly was blond and upbeat, a sunny counterpoint to the dark Salazar. She set school records in the 3000, 5000, and 10,000 meters, yet she hated competing. "It was just like school," she said. "I loved being with people, and learning, but I hated taking the tests."

Alberto was too intense for her at first — too obsessive about his training, too competitive with other runners — but he wore her down. Their initial relationship, however, was short-lived. She threw him over for pole-vaulter Tom Hintnaus, who would go on to become the iconic Calvin Klein underwear model photographed by Bruce Weber. Hintnaus's tanned and ripped body, leaning back against a whitewashed wall and clad only in his briefs, stopped traffic in Times Square when it went up as a billboard in 1982.

Alberto was crushed, and he used his disappointment to punish himself on the roads, running additional intervals behind Coach Dellinger's back. He also used it to confront his father and tell him he wasn't going to become a doctor; he was switching his major to marketing and finance. It would become a familiar pattern: facing down disappointment with confrontation, embracing pain as a reward for pushing himself faster and harder.

In the spring, the Oregon Ducks faced off against one of their archrivals, Washington State University, which boasted the great Kenyan runner Henry Rono. Rono was among the first wave of top African runners to leave his country to run for an American university, and he had set a string of world records in the distance events. But in the 5000 meters, Salazar outkicked Rono and won the race in a time of 13:42. It was a defining moment, right up there with beating Frank Shorter at Falmouth. But it was short-lived. A few weeks later, Rono beat him at the Pac-10 championships, and shortly thereafter came Salazar's crushing sixth-place finish in the 10,000 meters at the NCAA finals.

He was only a sophomore, with two more years of college eligibility and, from an objective viewpoint, plenty of time to conquer the world. His mentor, Bill Rodgers, had had an unremarkable college career, and it was only in Frank Shorter's senior year that he'd shown any promise. But Salazar was not patient, and he could not wait. He concluded that he had not pushed himself hard enough. Restraint was for mortals; he was a Salazar. He set his sights on the roads and swore he would never be broken again.

Bill Rodgers was accustomed to the young Turks who, every weekend, wanted to take him down. Once, he had been one of them. But now he was the Man. With Shorter laid up following surgery on his injured foot, Rodgers had the roads to himself. In 1978, he won twenty-seven of the thirty races he entered and set a world record in the ten kilometers on the road. He won the Pepsi 10,000-meter nationals and the New York City and Boston Marathons. If Salazar planned to take him down, he had his work cut out for him.

On February 16, 1978, distance running officially entered the public consciousness. No longer a sport for kooks and fanatics, the date marked the ascension of *The Complete Book of Running,* by Jim Fixx, to number one on the nonfiction bestseller list. It remained among the top ten for ninety-one weeks and sold more than a million copies, turning its author into a New Age prophet. Fixx had been overweight and a smoker, with a family history of heart disease, and he brought to the sport the convert's zeal and infatuation. With Fixx's sinewy legs in red short shorts gracing the cover, the book proclaimed musculature and fitness for all.

By the time of that summer's Falmouth Road Race, this ethos of mass participation had reached its apogee. Although the 1978 event boasted the most competitive field in any U.S. road race — perhaps ever — at times it seemed the public was less interested in the runners than in running. As the *Boston Globe* noted breathlessly, "The race took a back seat to the participatory aspect and just plain fun people had for themselves." At the opposite end, Kenny Moore, writing in *Sports Illustrated,* bemoaned the lack of fitness of most of the participants and claimed that "three-quarters of America's 25 million runners have run for two years or less."

It was Tommy Leonard's dream to turn the road into a street party, and he had succeeded. Yet he was in awe of athletes such as Shorter and Rodgers and still pinched himself at their presence. Like a true aficionado, he understood the virtuosity of greatness and drew inspiration from it. And he never ignored it. Until that summer, the Falmouth Road Race existed in a kind of equipoise between the elite and the masses, with the former providing motivation for the latter. The pendulum, however, had begun to swing.

The change did not go unnoticed by the elite athletes. While Bill Rodgers was as graceful as ever, others groused about the crowds, the starting line, the finishing area. Some even passed on Falmouth to race overseas or in venues where they would have the roads to themselves. The inexperience of most of the participants led the more seasoned runners to predict dire consequences in the midsummer heat and humidity. No one, of course, imagined that it would be an elite athlete who would succumb.

For Salazar, the crowds were a minor annoyance. As one of the top seeds, he was shuttled to the front of the starting line, and once the gun went off, he might as well have been in a separate race. Only the top-ranked women had to deal with the masses, as male runners jostled to keep pace with them on the roads or simply craved the exposure that running with the leaders gave them. It was not unusual to see the lead women surrounded by a pack of a dozen men, which was both irritating and distracting (and, because women were prohibited from being paced by men, potentially disqualifying). Yet Salazar had his share of admirers as well, younger runners mostly, who thought of him as Prefontaine's heir and craved his magic touch, or at least a nod of acknowledgment. He was polite but not warm, and acted as if he wished they would go away and let him run.

He spoke, instead, to Rudy Chapa, who had joined him on the

East Coast for the race, and to Nancy Robinson, the daughter of the race's medical director, whom he had started dating after Molly broke up with him. Both Nancy and Rudy were contenders in their own right, but even they knew this was Alberto's race. He was like a thoroughbred in a lather before the Kentucky Derby, practically seething with frustration over the NCAAs and amped for redemption. What better place to prove his mettle than in his backyard, where he had first raced as a boy and now returned as a man. It was the perfect recipe for disaster.

Salazar did not notice the heat. It was not the hottest day of the summer or even the hottest day on which the race had been run. The start time had been moved up two hours, to 10 a.m., and the sun was hidden behind the haze, creating the illusion of calm. Certainly, it wasn't as hot as Nebraska in July, when he had defeated Ralph King. But it was hot enough to cause discomfort, and the humidity was deceptive. At such high levels, it would prevent the body from cooling down, and on even a relatively mild day, it could become brutal. Later Chapa would observe, "I'd pour water on my head, and it felt like it was boiling by the time it hit my neck."

The local runners were used to the Cape's pea soup fog and knew that the sun would burn away the haze by late afternoon. This morning, however, it was particularly soupy. Because the hottest part of the race would be the flat strip along Surf Drive, they decided to hold back until they were safely under cover of the trees near Falmouth Harbor. It was the smart play, but it demanded more than a passing familiarity with the course. It also required an awareness of the risk and a sense of caution, neither of which Salazar possessed.

So when the gun sounded, he jumped to the front. As the pack took the first turn by the library, he was tucked in the first group. The only serious contender in front of him was Mike Roche, who would regret his early lead. Bill Rodgers was about a dozen places behind. They ran hard up the slight hill with the view of the Coast Guard station and turned right onto Church Street. Clackety-clack over the old wooden bridge. Past the Church of the Messiah, where a crowd of Sunday worshipers cheered them on. Then into the first downhill as they approached Nobska Beach. This was where Rodgers got his legs and moved to the front. A little surge, an imperceptible sprint, and he was there. Salazar felt him over his left shoulder and instinctively quickened his stride to keep pace.

A breeze blew off the water, fooling the runners into thinking it was cool. In fact, with little place for the moisture to go, the sweat just sat on their skin, failing to do much good. When they climbed the hill and disappeared into the woods behind the lighthouse, they were already overheated, their bodies trying to throw off heat on every exhaled breath.

Now the race began. The poseurs and charlatans had faded, and the serious runners moved to the front. There would never be another race like Falmouth, and never another Falmouth like 1978. Nineteen of the top twenty finishers were Americans, and each could win any race in the absence of the others. Men such as Salazar, Bruce Bickford, Greg Meyer, and Herb Lindsay would go on to illustrious careers, while Rodgers, Roche, Craig Virgin, Garry Bjorklund, Randy Thomas, Jeff Galloway, Ed Sheehan, and Amby Burfoot were already at the height of their careers. On the women's side, Joan Benoit would burst into public view, taking four minutes off her winning time in 1976, on her way to becoming the best female distance runner the United States has ever produced. But it wasn't just the depth of the field; it was the spirit of competition, the enthusiasm of the crowd, the dizzying thrill of a joy ride at its zenith when no one wants to look down.

In the woods, mini-rivalries erupted. Bob Hodge versus Randy Thomas. Bickford versus Meyer. Someone would take an extra-quick step or dart to his right, and the race was on. One man would grab for a cup of water, slosh it over his head, and then toss the cup to the road. Another would slide to the left while checking his watch, then slip back into the pack. They ran this way as they rose and descended, the road shaded and steamy, the air still and dank. The best against the better, the fast against the faster.

170

And then there were four: Rodgers, Roche, Virgin, and Salazar. Before them stretched a mile and a half of beach road: flat, fast, and dangerous. The sun beat down; the haze had dissipated; the wind at their backs did nothing to cool them. Rodgers pushed, and the others tried to respond. Roche slipped first. He had gone out too fast, and his legs felt heavy and dull. In the span of a few seconds, he was suddenly three strides behind. Then Rodgers surged again, and this time it was Virgin who faltered. After a month of racing in Europe, his calves were beat-up and sore. He throttled back, saving his energy for the battle for third.

Only Salazar would not let go. He was tired and hot, but he knew he was fit and fast. Winning was only a state of mind. He had lost at the NCAAs because he'd allowed himself to think he would lose. Now he forced those thoughts from his mind and concentrated on the road. He was mentally tougher than all his competitors, he believed. From his earliest days running around the house for Ricardo, to the twenty-mile he ran as a high school freshman, to the 5000 meters he ran on the Nebraska track, his greatest moments were the ones where he refused to acknowledge the possibility of defeat. What was the body but a servant of the mind, a slab of meat? It made no decisions and followed directions. He told it to go, and it went. His mind gave the orders, and his muscles flexed, his knees lifted, and his feet left the road behind.

Like every runner, Bill Rodgers had lost more races than he'd won. He knew the agony of defeat better than the thrill of victory, and although he wasn't inured to it, losing came with the territory. One man crossed the finish line first, and everyone else followed. He had been on a hot streak, but he'd always known this moment would arrive — just as the talented veteran catcher can feel his joints creaking as he looks into the dugout and sees the young buck strapping on his mask. Now here was Alberto Salazar, asking Rodgers if Bill wanted him to lead. Wasn't that what racing was about? Rodgers had said it himself: "taking down kings."

"Take it. It's yours," he said. He mentally prepared himself to be passed, gauging his ability to hold off Virgin and Roche for second place. It would be a letdown, but it was better than third. One defeat didn't mean the crown had been passed. Yet he had to fight the sense of loss at his changed circumstances, and what it might portend.

Rodgers kept his head down, his eyes focused on the road, but after a few seconds, there was no Alberto. He was a little perplexed, but he was concentrating more on holding his pace and his place. After about thirty seconds, he wondered what had happened to the younger runner. Yet it was a fleeting thought. He was still in first place, and the crowds were thick and raucous with supporters. There were two miles to go, and he had a race to run. He reached the end of Surf Drive, turned left away from the beach, and stretched his lead over his other rivals.

Meanwhile, Salazar's brain was sending instructions to his body, but his body was responding with its own, more primitive, language. As he lost water through perspiration, his capillaries squeezed out water from his blood to replace the lost fluid in his tissues. Because of the reduced blood volume, his blood pressure dropped. To maintain adequate pressure, his arteries constricted, keeping blood flowing to the brain but reducing the flow to his extremities. Without enough blood, his muscles lacked oxygen for energy and were impaired in their ability to excrete waste products such as carbon dioxide and lactic acid. Soon he began to stumble and weave across the road. Craig Virgin passed him, then so did Mike Roche. He dropped from second to fourth, to fifth, seventh, eighth, then tenth. Bob Hodge, who came upon him near the final hill into Falmouth Heights, thought he looked "wobbly" and unwell.

If he had stopped at that moment and drunk some fruit juice and water, he might have recovered. But no one knew he was on the verge of collapse. He just looked like a guy who had gone out too fast and faded. He himself was confused and disoriented. As he continued to perspire and lose even more water, his arteries constricted further, until eventually the blood flow to his brain was impeded.

That Salazar managed to run two miles in such a condition

172

was a testament to his mental toughness and stubborn will. It was also extremely perilous. By the time he reached the finish line, his body temperature had climbed to 108 degrees, nearly 10 degrees above normal, in the red zone where death usually followed. He had stopped perspiring entirely, and his skin was dry and papery. A race volunteer noticed him staggering through the finish chute and rushed to his side. The volunteer half carried, half dragged the young runner to the medical tent, where they were met by Dr. Arthur Crago.

Dr. Crago immediately recognized the symptoms of heat stroke. Salazar was ashen, wobbly, and weak. In preparation for that exact scenario, volunteers had filled several plastic tubs with ice and water. Now Dr. Crago steered Salazar to a tub and helped him step inside. Salazar got in, but he wasn't happy. In fact, he immediately started yelling and thrashing. This was common among heat stroke victims, who are disoriented and often combative, but it was also dangerous. He might hurt himself or one of the volunteers who were trying to help him. Worse, he might knock over the tub. The most urgent need was to bring his body temperature down so that he wouldn't suffer a seizure or brain damage, and the best way to do that was to keep him in ice water.

Dr. Arthur Robinson, the race's medical director, arrived, and Salazar greeted him with a string of expletives. Later, he would be mortified when he recalled his behavior. This was his girlfriend's father, and he was a good Catholic boy who did not curse like a fishmonger. But Dr. Robinson had seen heat stroke victims before and knew they could be belligerent. He listened calmly and reviewed his colleague's notes while the young man in his care cursed and groaned.

Then Salazar's father arrived, and the volume under the tent climbed a few notches. The runner's body temperature was actually coming down, but his father didn't trust the race doctors and insisted they send him to the hospital. Yet even a short trip in the ambulance could cause his body temperature to spike, with irreparable consequences. The best treatment was for him to remain in the ice bath until his temperature normalized. But José Salazar insisted, his voice growing louder and his gestures more animated. Finally, an ambulance was called. By the time it appeared, Salazar's temperature had dropped to 102, which was safe enough to transport him to the ER. The doctors wheeled him on a gurney into the custody of the paramedics, who took off for Falmouth Hospital with sirens blaring and José Salazar wailing, or vice versa.

Several hours later, as the Brothers Four rocked and rolled, the beer-soaked guests were treated to a surprise visitor. Alberto Salazar strolled inside, walking stiffly but cockily. He showed off the puncture wounds in his arm where nurses had inserted the IV and answered the questions of his inebriated fellow athletes. Yes, it was true he had nearly died. Yes, it was true his father had called a priest, who had given him last rites. But here he was, alive and well, and ready to run again.

Tommy Leonard poured him a beer, while former teammates shook his hand. Then the crowd gathered around and drank a toast to Falmouth, the fairest race in the land. The jukebox kicked on, and the dancing began. Before long, the old-timers were doing the jitterbug, and Tommy was singing along.

Salazar didn't dance. He stood apart, near the bar, reflecting on his race. He hadn't won, and he had nearly died. Yet a grim feeling of satisfaction — call it happiness — suffused him. He had not given up, even when his body begged for rest. He had run through death and emerged on the other side. There were no shining lights or heavenly music, no flashbacks or lasting regrets. But there were angels, and they watched over him. He believed that now.

Run, Alberto, they said. *Run.*

No more room on the press truck at the start
of the 1979 Falmouth Road Race.

Courtesy Falmouth Historical Society

15

Foreign Footsteps (1979)

> I grew up like a white Kenyan.
> — CRAIG VIRGIN

AS THE DECADE ENDED, Americans were firmly ensconced at the top of the running pyramid. Bill Rodgers was ranked number one in the world in the marathon. Craig Virgin was ranked number two in the 10,000 meters, as was Marty Liquori in the 5000 meters. Steve Scott and Don Paige were ranked third and seventh, respectively, in the 1500 meters. In the wings were Herb Lindsay, Kirk Pfeffer, Tony Sandoval, and Alberto Salazar, among other talented lights. Frank Shorter was recovering from foot surgery and back problems, but he was clearly considered a top seed for the upcoming Moscow Olympics. In fact, it appeared that the United States had a very good chance of taking gold, silver, and bronze in the marathon at the 1980 games.

Yet the seeds of change had been planted before Shorter ever set foot on a track. On the eastern coast of Africa, along the equatorial rim, runners from Ethiopia, Kenya, and Tanzania emerged from colonial rule to claim a place on the champions' podium. They gave hope to a younger generation of athletes who would eventually supplant their American rivals. Although the debate continues to rage over what makes African distance runners so good, there are no genetic or racial mysteries here. Instead, the answer is the same across continents: a group of like-minded athletes bound together in a culture that fosters their sport.

When Ethiopia was liberated by the Allies in 1941, the government began building its own military, particularly an air force and the Imperial Guard. It was helped by Sweden, which sent aircraft and ex–military personnel to assist Emperor Haile Selassie. Among those who traveled to Addis Ababa was Onni Niskanen, a Swede who had been born in Finland, the homeland of the great Paavo Nurmi. Niskanen was a former middle-distance and cross-country runner who was said to be so devoted to athletics that his first wife demanded he choose between her and sports. Fortunately (for Ethiopia but not his wife), he chose sports. His job, as he later described it, was to "introduce Ethiopia to the Olympic community," a tall order in a country without any athletic organizations, sports infrastructure, or coaches.

Nevertheless, Niskanen cultivated contacts in the Olympic community in London in 1948 and began organizing competitions in Ethiopia, in which he offered up his old trophies as prizes. Distance running, he believed, was a natural fit for a people who were accustomed to running, because it was their normal means of transportation. Workers typically jogged to and from work, often carrying food or other items in small bundles strapped to their backs. It was also a practical decision in a country without stadiums or money for decent sports equipment. But at first, Niskanen had trouble getting his charges to do any organized training. They soon realized, however, that winning races could get them good jobs in the military or with the police, and that was all the inspiration they needed.

It was at the Imperial Guard Cadet School that Niskanen met Abebe Bikila. Bikila had won a place at the school by playing *yegena chewata*, a game favored by shepherds that resembles long-distance

178

hockey, with curved sticks and a wooden ball. Goalposts could be in different villages several miles apart. After seeing Bikila run, Niskanen was determined to turn him into an Olympic champion. He introduced the young Ethiopian to interval workouts and vitamin supplements and helped him relax his running style. (Niskanen said he ran like a "drilling soldier.")

Bikila quickly distinguished himself under Niskanen's training. In his second marathon, he not only defeated national long-distance legend Wami Biratu, but he ran three minutes faster than the winning time at the previous Olympic Games. As a result, he qualified for the Ethiopian team at the 1960 Rome Olympics. Yet he arrived at the games as an unknown. The first thing sportswriters noticed about him was that he ran barefoot, which they assumed was because of his extreme poverty and poor training. In fact, Bikila was used to running that way. The soles of his feet were thick and black, and one competitor compared them to "the tires of big military trucks." He tried to find running shoes in Rome to compete on the roads, but the ones he used gave him blisters, so he went without them.

The Olympic marathon began at 5:30 p.m. on a beautiful sunny day in September. The sight of the barefooted Ethiopian runner caused snickers and amusement among the throng gathered to watch the start, none of whom took him seriously. When the race began, however, Bikila attached himself to the Russian favorite in the second pack through the first five kilometers. Soon after, he moved into the group of four leaders and stayed there. At eighteen kilometers, the Moroccan champion, Rhadi Ben Abdesselam, threw in a surge, and Bikila was the only runner who went with him. The two men ran side by side over the next twelve kilometers as race announcers struggled over the correct pronunciation of Bikila's name. About two kilometers from the finish, Bikila took off, and Abdesselam could not go with him. He crossed the finish line in 2:15:16.2, a new world record.

Bikila's victory was stunning. It came on a course in the city

179

where Mussolini had celebrated his conquest over Addis Ababa only twenty-four years earlier. Not only was he the first black African to win an Olympic gold medal in any sport, but he seemed to have emerged from nowhere. (He also remains the only barefoot runner ever to win an Olympic medal.) Although Niskanen trumpeted his ability, no one had paid any attention to the crazy Swede and his barefoot protégé. That quickly changed.

After the Olympics, Bikila went on a tear, winning twelve of his next thirteen marathons. At the Tokyo Olympics in 1964, he won his second gold medal and set another world record, despite having had an appendectomy just a few weeks earlier. He became the most widely known and admired African on the continent, and when he died at the age of forty-one, the result of a cerebral hemorrhage stemming from a traffic accident four years earlier that had left him a quadriplegic, the world mourned.

Despite his untimely death, his medals signaled the emergence of African runners on the international stage and influenced a young Kenyan runner to take to the track at the middle distances. Like Bikila, Kipchoge "Kip" Keino developed as an athlete when he joined the police academy organized by his country's former occupiers. Within three years, he had qualified for a place on the Kenyan team at the British Empire and Commonwealth Games in Australia. Two years later, at the 1964 Tokyo Olympics, he improved his fastest time in the 5000 meters by twenty-five seconds and finished fifth. It was in Tokyo that he bought an orange baseball cap that became his signature. He would wear it in races and throw it off when he sprinted for the finish. It was a flamboyant touch that otherwise seemed out of character for a man whom competitors described as "shy and disarming."

Yet he was an aggressive runner, who thrived in competition and ran his best races when he had to fight for the lead. In 1965, he set world records in the 3000 and 5000 meters and missed the record in the mile by 0.1 second, running it in 3:54.2 and becoming the first African to break four minutes. He won two gold medals at the All-Africa Games and three at the 1966 British Empire and Commonwealth Games. But it was at the Mexico City Olympics in 1968 that he truly came to prominence.

Keino had entered himself in three events — the 1500, 5000, and 10,000 meters. Including heats, this meant he had to run six races in eight days. However, he arrived at the games with an undiagnosed gallbladder infection. In his first race, the 10,000, he collapsed in pain with three laps to go. Yet two days later, he came back and took silver in the 5000, losing by only two-tenths of a second. His last chance for gold was in the 1500 meters — the metric mile — where his main competition was Jim Ryun, the U.S. and world record holder. Ryun had not lost a mile race in three years and was fresh, while Keino was sick and had already run five races.

As if those were not obstacles enough, Ryun was famous for his devastating kick. That meant Keino, in his weakened condition, would have to go out hard and fast in order to hold off Ryun in the closing meters. It seemed an insurmountable task. Yet Keino ran his first lap in 56 seconds and went through the half-mile in 1:55.3, a world record pace. At altitude, in the thin air of Mexico City, he ran his third lap in 58 seconds. With two hundred meters to go, Keino had a twelve-meter lead. Ryun kicked, but Keino did not falter, and he did not let up. He crossed the line in 3:34.9, a new Olympic record. In fact, he had run the second half of the race faster than the first half, and if he had been able to maintain his pace for the full mile distance (about another 120 yards), he would have broken Ryun's world record for the event.

Keino continued to rack up victories in middle-distance events over the next several years. By the time of the Munich Olympics, however, he faced competition from another East African. Filbert Bayi was raised in the shadow of Mount Kilimanjaro in Arusha, Tanzania, and spent his early years running, sometimes as much as eight miles each way to school. Kip Keino was his boyhood idol, and he tried to emulate the older runner. At seventeen, he moved to Dar es Salaam to work as an air force technician while training in the hot and humid city. His speed workouts often consisted of sprinting alongside a belching diesel bus, then resting while passengers got on and off the bus. While this was certainly an unconventional method of interval training, he qualified for the 1972 Olympics in both the steeplechase and the 1500 meters.

Today we think of East Africans as distance runners, but at Munich — where Shorter won the marathon — Kenyans placed third in the 400 and 800 meters, second in the 1500 meters, and first in the 3000-meter steeplechase. Alas, while Keino was responsible for two of the Kenyan medals (gold in the steeplechase and silver in the 1500), Bayi was boxed in while racing and unable to get outside the pack to move on the leaders. Determined to avoid this fate in future races, Bayi developed his signature racing style — "seemingly suicidal front-running," as *Sports Illustrated* called it. He would take the lead at the very beginning of a race, opening a wide gap between himself and the rest of the pack, and either go down in flames or win in spectacular fashion. While runners generally consider such showboating to be bad manners, Bayi was not being rude; he just felt more comfortable out front. And the fans loved it. With Bayi in the race, they knew it would always be exciting.

His most famous race, and one of the most exciting track events ever, was the 1500 meters at the 1974 British Commonwealth Games in Christchurch, New Zealand. In a field that included the Kenyan Ben Jipcho and the New Zealanders Rod Dixon and John Walker, Bayi was out front from the gun, leading by as much as twenty meters until the last lap. As Jipcho and Walker closed in, Bayi fought them off, holding his lead and breaking Jim Ryun's world record in the process. The pace was so fast that the next four finishers' times were all within the top ten times ever. That race was also the beginning of a long rivalry between Bayi and Walker that took them across continents and made both men famous.

Later in his life, Bayi became a marathoner. His debut came in 1979 against Bill Rodgers and Alberto Salazar in New York City.

But while he was preparing for New York, a fellow East African, the Kenyan Hillary Tuwei, was leading another African charge — into American universities — along with his countryman, Henry Rono, who was Salazar's fierce rival. The year before, Rono had broken four world records in a span of eighty-one days. Tuwei had finished sixth in the 1978 Falmouth Road Race and was considered one of the top contenders in 1979.

The Africans had discovered that the American university system was a welcoming place where they could live and eat for free, while forward-thinking U.S. coaches saw a vast, untapped pool of runners who could jolt their programs with an influx of talent. In the years to come, schools such as Washington State University, Villanova, and the University of Texas at El Paso would rise in the rankings as a result of this win-win scenario.

Falmouth 1979, however, was not to be the Africans' breakthrough year. That would come in 1983 — appropriately enough, at the end of the decade that defined the boom. Instead, 1979 was all red, white, and blue — but not because of Shorter, Rodgers, or Salazar.

Shorter was running well after his foot surgery. He placed third behind Rodgers and Virgin in the Trevira Twosome in New York and beat Rodgers in races in Colorado and Chicago. Rodgers won Boston for the third time, breaking his own U.S. record. Salazar beat Rono in the NCAA cross-country championships, claiming his first individual title, and took All-American honors in the 10,000 meters.

But Falmouth 1979 belonged to the non-marathoners, the track and road men whose leg speed was better suited for that distance. Craig Virgin was the U.S. record holder in the 10,000 meters, a race that was almost the same length as Falmouth. Herb Lindsay had recently set the U.S. record in the ten-mile. Although Rodgers was the sentimental favorite and Tommy Leonard's pick to win, it was Virgin, then Lindsay, who crossed the line before Boston Billy, while Shorter finished fifth. Virgin's time broke Rodgers's course record by two seconds. As proof of the depth of the field, the first seven runners finished within twenty-six seconds of one another.

Rodgers, always the statesman, congratulated the victors and said he would have to try harder next year. Shorter declared himself satisfied with the quick pace. Neither man attributed any significance to the moment. Indeed, Rodgers would go on to win the New York City Marathon a few months later. But the two runners would never win Falmouth again. The 1979 race signaled, as Virgin said later, "a changing of the guard."

Across the country another young runner was coming into his own, while across the ocean an entire continent was stirring. The footsteps were falling as the clock ticked down.

Alberto Salazar pulling away from Rodolfo Gómez
on Fifth Avenue in Salazar's debut marathon.

Associated Press

16

A Brave New World (1980)

I got my revenge. I became a Republican that year.

— DON PAIGE

WHEN SOVIET TANKS rolled into Afghanistan in December 1979, Shorter, Rodgers, and Salazar did not pay much attention. All were deeply involved in training for the U.S. Olympic trials and the 1980 Olympics in Moscow. Rodgers was still peeved about his terrible race at Montreal and craved a second chance. He was the world's top-ranked marathoner and had been ruling the roads for the past two years. Yet he couldn't shake the insecurity that came from lacking a gold medal. As fast as he ran, as many times as he beat Shorter, the Yalie still had his gold and his silver. Moscow would be Rodgers's opportunity to vanquish his demons. Although Shorter was injured again and had run badly in New York, no one counted him out — least of all himself. As for Salazar, he had yet to run a marathon and wasn't going to start with the Olympics. Instead, as the NCAA Division I cross-country champion, he set his sights on the 10,000 meters. The marathon would have to wait.

A boycott of the games was initially suggested by Rolf Pauls of West Germany at an emergency NATO meeting in Brussels. It was supported by President Jimmy Carter, who decided that boycotting the Olympics would be an effective method of condemning the Soviet Union's invasion without taking military action. Like Germany in 1936, the Soviet Union was using the games to showcase its political system, with athletic achievement intended to demonstrate the strengths and successes of communism. A boycott was a rejection of this overly simplistic equation and denied the Communists their moment to shine.

Through the U.S. Olympic Committee, Carter lobbied the International Olympic Committee to move, reschedule, or cancel the games. The IOC rejected the proposal, and so Carter stepped up his efforts domestically, exhorting Congress, the American people, and the athletes themselves not to condone the Soviets' actions. Finally, thanks largely to a speech by Vice President Walter Mondale that included moral and patriotic appeals, the USOC House of Delegates voted for a boycott.

The reaction from the athletes was immediate and nearly universally condemnatory. Rodgers claimed the United States was afraid of the Soviets' athletic superiority. "We are simply a tool, an implement," he said. "No one cares at all, until we can be used for their purposes." His anger spilled onto the front page of the *Boston Globe,* which ran the headline MARATHON MAN TURNS ANGRY YOUNG MAN the week before the Boston Marathon. In a snub of the USOC, he decided not to run in the Olympic trials — rejecting the idea of solidarity for political expediency — in order to run Boston, which he won for the fourth straight time. He was now the only runner to achieve four victories in both the New York City and Boston Marathons, and he felt cheated by his country's refusal to honor his coronation. It was another betrayal by a government he didn't trust, and he never forgave President Carter for this decision.

Shorter was oddly stoic about the boycott. He thought it was wrong "from every perspective," as he later wrote, but he claimed to be "naïve in such matters." If the president said the national interest was at stake, he took the president at his word. By this time, however, Shorter knew he was not going to recover from his injuries in time to run a decent marathon at Moscow. In fact, he ran the trials but finished twenty-seventh, more than fifteen minutes slower than his qualifying time in 1976. There was little for him to gain by protesting the boycott, and although he could be fierce in defense of his interests — witness his efforts in attacking the amateur system — he had little interest in fighting against the Olympic boycott.

As for Salazar, he was redshirted for what would have been his last college track season in order to spend a month in Kenya preparing for the 10,000 meters. "For a national class runner," he wrote in *14 Minutes,* "the Olympics are the only real game in town. [They're] how you establish your reputation, and if you're a professional, that's how you make your real money." But he ended up injured for most of the spring and barely recovered in time to finish third in the event at the trials. The race was won by Craig Virgin, who set a U.S. record and ran the second-fastest time in the world. Both men "qualified" for the Olympics, but it was an empty honor. They were Olympic athletes without a venue, world-class competitors who could not compete against the world.

In the end, sixty-five countries did not attend the Moscow games. Some participated in the hastily constructed Olympic Boycott Games in Philadelphia (officially called the Liberty Bell Classic). As a concession prize, American athletes were given a congressional medal that miler Steve Scott called garbage. "It was like, 'OK we're not going to let you go to the Olympics so we're going to give you these fake gold medals,'" he said. A small group of athletes, led by rower Anita DeFrantz, decided to sue the USOC for breach of the Amateur Sports Act of 1978. The suit was dismissed by a federal appellate court. Another group planned to race anyway by sneaking into Moscow from Hungary on buses. When the Secret Service found out about their plans, it threatened to confiscate the passport of any American athlete who attempted to compete. Even those who supported the boycott — or at least understood it — came to feel embittered and angry by the empty gesture. As swimmer Craig Beardsley said, "If it was going to do some good, then we could sacrifice. But as time went on, as we realized what little impact it had, I became angry for what the boycott did to all these people, my friends and teammates, and people in all those other countries too."

Shorter already had his medals, but Rodgers and Salazar did not, and it turned out they would never get them. Nearly half the members of the 1980 U.S. Olympic team never made another squad, including both runners. Indeed, in 1984 the Soviet Union and East Germany boycotted the Los Angeles Olympics in reprisal, and as a result, an entire generation of athletes was denied the opportunity to compete on the biggest stage against the best international competition. The boycott might not have changed the course of political events, but it shattered the dreams of nearly every athlete who did not compete.

For Alberto Salazar, however, the boycott was a blessing in disguise. He had used up his four years of college eligibility for cross-country, and the months loomed emptily in front of him. Over the summer, he raced in Europe, setting personal bests in the 5000 and 10,000 meters, but a strained hamstring sent him back to Eugene with his second serious injury in six months. This was a warning to slow down, but Salazar ignored it. Even his cross-training was intense: he once suffered hypothermia when he swam for too long in Coach Dellinger's unheated pool in February. If death could not stop him, a soft-tissue injury certainly couldn't either. So when a short, foreign-looking man made him an offer, Salazar could not refuse.

Fred Lebow had traveled to Oregon to recruit America's next great distance star to run in the New York City Marathon. He knew about Salazar's desire to tackle the distance — it was no great secret — and he also knew that without the glory of the Olympics or a fall season in front of him, Salazar would need a challenge. Like the best salesman, he played to the customer's desires. The moment was ripe for a new champion, Lebow said, someone who could wrest the crown from Bill Rodgers. He knew Salazar could be that runner.

It was an intoxicating prophecy, and it had its desired effect. The marathon had been Salazar's dream since the day he saw Rodgers leading at Boston, and now the man who held the keys to New York City was offering them to him. New York was the perfect place for Salazar's debut: it was brash, new, and bold. Like the runner himself, the New York City Marathon was the bright light in a resurgent distance event and offered no apologies for muscling its way to the front. It did not create the boom, but like the Falmouth Road Race, it was born of the moment and lifted running to new heights. It was the stage on which America announced its newfound obsession to the world and on which its stars would shine. And of all the lights in the firmament, none would shine brighter than Alberto Salazar.

Coach Bill Squires had instructed Salazar to wait until he was older and stronger before attempting the marathon. But Dellinger — who had never trained a world-class marathoner, and whose restraint was about as strong as a piece of chewing gum — thought he could do it, and that was all Salazar needed. It was true he hadn't logged the mileage that might normally be expected of a marathoner, but both he and Dellinger believed the marathon could be approached as a long road race. Most of the miles a marathoner ran in training were junk anyway — long slow distance that served no purpose except to circulate blood to the legs. Salazar didn't believe in LSD. Everything he ran was fast and hard. What he lacked in mileage he more than made up for in strength and speed. At his best, he never ran more than 151 miles a week (despite reports that had him running more than 200), but many of those miles were at or near race pace. One of Dellinger's favorite workouts was to have the runners tackle the first 200 meters of a 400-meter track loop in 30 seconds (a four-minute-mile pace), then slow to 40 seconds for the next 200 meters, and then repeat. Salazar's teammates would run eight to ten sets. Salazar did fourteen. Another workout had them running three progressively faster 400-meter intervals on the track at 70 seconds,

65 seconds, and 60 seconds, then jogging up the Thirtieth Avenue hill in Eugene and running a three-quarter-mile in 3:05, and then returning to the track for three more 400-meter intervals. Most runners would do one set. The better runners would do two. Salazar did three.

Because of his injured hamstring, he had only about six good weeks of training before New York. Once again, however, this probably worked to his advantage. Left to his own devices, he would have stepped up his mileage and run himself into the ground. Instead, he didn't have enough time to get injured again. He barely had enough time to run his favorite workouts, shower, and then hop a plane for New York.

He arrived on Thursday night before the Sunday race. He flew by himself, without a coach or support team. At the prerace press conference, dressed in a black motorcycle jacket, he responded to a reporter's question by stating that "barring the unforeseen, I should run under 2:10." Later, he attributed the prediction to Lebow, but the truth was, it originated with him. Only one American had ever run under 2:10, and now here was a twenty-two-year-old college kid, a rookie, predicting he would be the second. The press ate it up. With his dark good looks, his black jacket, and his prediction of greatness, he became, in his own words, "a distance-running version of Joe Namath or Muhammad Ali." New Yorkers loved a little chutzpah, and Salazar's unwitting trash talk was a colorful contrast to the more subdued tones of Frank Shorter, Bill Rodgers, and Grete Waitz, the women's marathon champion, a Norwegian who had won the hearts of New Yorkers despite being so damned polite. His father shared his outlook, telling reporters his son would win. "He has always called the outcome, and he has always done it," José Salazar said.

Alberto would spend the rest of his life denying that he was arrogant. If the word means "having an exaggerated opinion of one's own ability," he was not. He never bragged or boasted; he simply stated the truth as he saw it, and he was usually correct. His prediction in New York was based on his (and Dellinger's) rational evaluation of his fitness level. To the extent *arrogance* means "a feeling of superiority," the word comes closer to capturing his personality. He did believe he was faster, tougher, and better than any other runner on the roads. He had run through death at Falmouth; what could stop him? Yet self-confidence was a trait of every successful athlete, without which it would be difficult to win.

But if *arrogant* is defined as "proud, disdainful, or aloof," then Salazar fit the bill. He saw no reason for niceties and lacked both Shorter's patrician polish and Rodgers's gee-whiz openness. He had no time for stupid questions (or questions he thought were stupid) and no patience for distractions that diverted him from his goal of being the best distance runner in the world.

In truth, this was a learned defense mechanism, born of insecurity and augmented by depression. By his own admission, it was easier to focus on his running than to deal with the feelings of social unease that often plagued him. His inchoate anger at his father, and the feelings of despair he couldn't name, were more simply directed outward at inept reporters, ineffectual race directors, and anyone else who provided an easy target. This made him arrogant, but it was an arrogance tinged with sadness, a protective skin to cover wounds he could not heal.

Of course, Salazar's prediction irritated Bill Rodgers. Rodgers was, after all, the course and U.S. record holder, the only American who had, in fact, run under 2:10. Although he had been beaten at Falmouth that summer by the New Zealander Rod Dixon, the first foreign runner to win the race, Rodgers was the only man to have won the New York City Marathon four times in a row. He had followed Salazar's progress and knew of his exploits at the Olympic trials and in Europe. But even if Salazar had not been injured and limited in his training, a road race was a different beast than the measured cadence of the track, and a marathon was another order beyond that. "There are twenty miles out there after Alberto is used to stopping," he said. "He's going to learn something in them. No rookie is going to beat me."

October 26, 1980, dawned cold and blustery in New York. Salazar had taken his younger brother for pizza at one in the morning and had had only a few hours of sleep. Nevertheless, the buzz of nervous energy burned off any fatigue. He hopped out of bed before the alarm sounded and dressed in the dark for the short trip to Staten Island. He was headed there by car, but he would be returning on foot.

At race time, it was 45 degrees, with the wind gusting to thirty-five miles an hour. Fortunately, the gusts were at the runners' backs at the starting line. As they peered over the expanse of the Verrazano Bridge, the crowd of 14,000 runners huddled together for warmth and made do with garbage bags, sheets, or old sweatshirts they planned to discard as soon as the gun sounded. There is always an electric current of excitement before a major race begins, but there was something special in the air that October morning. The two best distance runners in the world were facing off, and the crowd behind them practically pulsed with collective anticipation. This was the Olympic moment that had eluded America, the bearing of the torch that symbolized the country's embrace of the running boom. Salazar's youth was the boom's bright future, while Rodgers's experience highlighted its present. There was no one in the crowd who hadn't heard Salazar's brash prediction, and no one without an opinion about its merit. The runners had come to test their own bodies, but they also wanted a race. They were about to get one.

When the gun went off, the runners snaked over the Verrazano Bridge, below a phalanx of helicopters and above a coterie of fireboats spraying fountains into the air. Fank Nenshun of China took an early lead, with Salazar and Rodgers in a large pack that included Filbert Bayi, making his marathon debut, not far behind.

The runners knew to conserve their energy over the first twenty miles in the hope of having something left for the last six. The wind gave them an added push, making the 4:52 pace feel "easy," as Salazar later said. After three miles, Bayi pulled into the lead along with two countrymen. Although it seemed a brash move for a novice, Bayi was a serious competitor and couldn't be ignored. Both Rodgers and Salazar kept him close.

At seven miles, the front pack had thirty runners. At ten miles, Salazar pulled up alongside Rodgers and noted that the race felt easy. "Don't worry, rookie," said the older man, "your time will come."

By the halfway point, the pack had dwindled to about twenty. At fourteen miles, Dick Beardsley stumbled on a pothole and fell. It might have gone unnoticed — an anonymous casualty of any urban distance race — except he took Rodgers down with him. While Beardsley got up quickly and resumed racing, Rodgers lay prone for several seconds longer and lost eighty yards on the leaders. Suddenly, the front pack was drastically rearranged. At sixteen miles, it consisted of Salazar, John Graham of England, and Rodolfo Gómez of Mexico, the silver medalist in the 1980 Olympic marathon, with a second pack strung out over a quarter mile behind.

Salazar still felt loose and was tempted to go, but he remembered the race would really begin in the last six miles. So he bided his time behind Gómez and Graham. At eighteen miles, he felt a stitch in his side. He tried to relax, concentrating on exhaling deep, even breaths, but the stitch stayed with him. Nineteen miles. Twenty miles. Still there. A harbinger of doom or just a kink to work out? But right before twenty-one miles, as suddenly as it had come on, the stitch disappeared. Salazar picked up the pace, and Graham was gone. Now it was just Gómez, about two strides in front, as the race approached Central Park. Salazar moved to the Mexican's shoulder and stayed there, letting Gómez ponder what he really had left. He felt totally in control and ready to pounce, waiting for his moment to wrest the lead from the Olympic medalist.

Up ahead there was a water station, about four miles from the finish line. When Gómez slowed to grab a cup, Salazar made his break. He took off, leaving Gómez about forty yards behind, his lead increasing with each stride. With three miles to go, Salazar had a hundred-yard lead. As he came down the hill to the southern end of Central Park, the spectators roared their encouragement. Gómez was fading, Salazar was sprinting, and it looked like New York would have a new marathon champion.

Around the park and up the final hill by Tavern on the Green, Salazar was all alone and running like a man possessed. He broke the tape in 2:09:41, eclipsing Rodgers's course record by twenty-eight seconds and running the second-fastest marathon ever by an American, and the fastest first marathon by anyone. Gómez finished second, followed by Graham, Jeff Wells of Texas, and then Rodgers, who finished in 2:13:21. On the women's side, Grete Waitz won her third New York City Marathon (on her way to accumulating nine victories in the race) and set her third world record on the course, running it in 2:25:42.

"The Rookie" had done what he'd predicted and beaten Rodgers at his own game on the field he had called his second home. It was Alberto Salazar's moment, his first victory over Bill Rodgers and the rising of his star. Yet when reporters asked him how he felt, he shrugged and replied that he was not impressed. There was no magic in the numbers and nothing special about the marathon. It was just another race on the roads. "I don't think I proved anything to myself," he said. "But I imagine I did to a lot of others."

The comment did not earn him many friends in the running community, including Bill Rodgers, who thought the kid should have more respect for the distance. Salazar had beaten him on the roads today, but Rodgers still had the U.S. record and the better résumé. Next time, things would be different.

But the United States had a new champion for a new decade, a swaggering upstart perfect for the shifting mood of a nation that was shrugging off the doldrums with a new president who promised it was "morning in America." As proof, on the day of his inauguration, Ronald Reagan announced the release of the American hostages in Iran, who had been held for 444 days. In the Salazar family, as in many other families across the land, there was much rejoicing. Reagan's jingoistic fervor and self-help credo were a welcome antidote to Democratic despondency. For too long, the country had apologized for its outsize appetite and hung its collective head in shame. It was time to kick some ass.

Alberto Salazar was just the runner to do it.

Alberto Salazar breaks the world record
at the New York City Marathon.

New York Daily News via Getty Images

17

The King Is Dead. Long Live the King. (1981)

My mother said I came out running.

— ROD DIXON

I T WAS TOMMY LEONARD'S tradition to hand the winner a beer at the finish line in Falmouth Heights. Not that it was the first thing every runner wanted, but it was the first thing Tommy thought the winner *should* want. If running was an excuse for drinking, then running fast was an excuse for drinking more. It was all in good fun, as the Kiwi Rod Dixon learned after he won the race in 1980, beating out Herb Lindsay, who finished second for a second straight year, and Bill Rodgers, who dropped to sixteenth. "Bring Dixon beer!" went the cheer. And so Tommy did.

The race had grown significantly since its beginnings as a hangover cure along the shore. In 1981, it was voted Best USA Road Race by *Runner's World,* beating out the Boston and New York City Marathons. Tommy continued to hand out beers, but whispers about his drinking followed him around. Passing out in a bathtub didn't seem like that much fun, at least to people who cared about these things, and they tried to keep a closer eye on Tommy.

A new sense of earnestness came with the accolades, and as the Falmouth Road Race and the running boom became more "professionalized," men like Tommy found themselves marginalized. Tommy was a colorful "character," to be sure. But sponsors such as Perrier, New Balance, and Nike had begun to sink real money into running, and they wanted a return on their investment, not a toga party. By the early 1980s, Tommy's role became that of meeter and greeter, while the real work happened elsewhere.

There were tensions, as well, between co–race directors Rich Sherman and John Carroll and their wives, Kathy and Lucia. Carroll, the track coach, handled the elite athletes and considered himself a connoisseur of their performances. Sherman, who had gone into the insurance business, was the organizer and moneyman. But each was strong willed, each considered himself responsible for the success of the race, and neither was willing to let go of any responsibility. They divvied up the jobs and mostly stayed out of each other's way, but there were places where they could not avoid conflict — especially as race day approached and the pressure mounted to seamlessly move thousands of people seven miles down the road. In the end, their four-way partnership managed to survive thirty-five years, until it collapsed from the weight of silence and long-suffered slights.

But all that was ahead of them in the glorious year of 1981. The year of Alberto Salazar.

The year began, auspiciously enough, with Salazar's engagement to Molly Morton. Although he failed to win the NCAAs in the spring, he was the Pac-10 champion in the 5000 and 10,000 meters and the reigning New York City Marathon winner. In the summer, he hired an agent from IMG and signed a sponsorship deal with Nike, which paid him a base salary of $50,000, plus several hundred thousand in incentives and bonuses for various achievements. It was rumored to be the highest sum ever offered to a distance runner at that time.

Salazar was the fortunate beneficiary of the path blazed by Shorter and Rodgers, and he peaked at just the right moment. The movie

Chariots of Fire was the surprise winner at the Academy Awards, earning five Oscars, including one for best picture. Fourteen thousand people ran the New York City Marathon in the fall, and the event was broadcast live nationally on ABC. Overseas, the inaugural running of the London Marathon, organized by Roger Bannister's former training partner, Chris Brasher, attracted 7,500 entrants and was won by an American, Dick Beardsley. Running, and runners, had never been more popular, and Salazar was the most popular of them all. The gangly kid from Wayland who couldn't get a prom date was now the hottie from Oregon, his dance card booked well into the night.

It is easy, in hindsight, to look at an era and say this is where it ends. Both Bill Rodgers and Frank Shorter believed they were still at the top of their game. They had struggled of late, but Rodgers had recently won the Houston Marathon and the Pepsi Challenge 10k. Shorter won the 1981 Bolder Boulder, a ten-kilometer road race he had helped found in Colorado (which is now one of the biggest road races in the United States), and beat Rodgers in the inaugural Classic 10k in his hometown of Middletown, New York. Both men were talking to the press about the 1984 Los Angeles Olympics, and both planned to compete for a place on the U.S. team.

In fact, however, they were on the other side of a steady downward slide. Shorter was no longer ranked in the top ten in any distance event, and Rodgers had dropped to seventh in the marathon. Shorter had not won a marathon since the Olympic trials in 1976, and after Houston, Rodgers would never win another major U.S. marathon again. Both men were also going through turmoil in their personal lives and would soon divorce amid rumors of financial collapse and scandal.

The former Ellen Lalone had supported Rodgers and paid their bills while he was just a skinny space cadet shuffling through the snowdrifts. She had played bad cop when race directors came calling. And she had managed their business while he was on the road. Now, as their marriage disintegrated, she didn't want a pound of flesh (he needed it), but she would take 50 percent of his assets and tie him up in litigation for years. When the ink was finally dry on their divorce papers, Rodgers's running apparel business was in bankruptcy, and all but one of his stores had closed. (The last one would close in 2012.)

As for Louise Shorter, she had supported Frank from the beginning, traveled (and moved) across the country with him, convinced her parents to pay for his airfare when he couldn't afford it. But the regular absences created tension, as did a home with two small children, Frank's struggle with injuries, and his disputes with business partners. He was in constant demand, with his fair share of running groupies, and their marriage could not survive the temptations.

In contrast, Alberto Salazar had the brash arrogance of youth, born of the belief in his own immortality. When he announced his return to New York for his second attempt at the marathon, he boldly proclaimed that he would break Derek Clayton's twelve-year-old world record. He knew how close Bill Rodgers had gotten to the record, and he knew he was faster than his old training partner. His inaugural attempt at the distance had been "easy," and there was no reason to think he couldn't lop another sixty-eight seconds off his time.

Rodgers begged to differ. "Al's going to find it's different, being in demand," he told the *Boston Globe*'s Joe Concannon. "It's a much easier situation he was in [last year], being a student. It's much more conducive to a good performance to be coming off a track season, to be a student." Then he reminded the *Globe*'s readers that he was a student, too, when he won his first Boston Marathon.

Rodgers found it irritating that the media bathed Salazar in glory while portraying him as a "mercenary" simply because he said that he deserved to be paid. Why shouldn't he make a living from his sport? "I put in a lot more effort than a golfer," he told *Boston* magazine. "On a calorie chart, playing a round of golf is probably equivalent to playing a game of canasta." And don't get him started on baseball or football. "It nauseates me that someone like [Joe]

Namath is held up to all the kids in this country as a great athlete," he said. Tossing a football in a straight line was nothing compared to the physical rigors of distance running.

But he saved his real wrath for Fred Lebow and U.S. road race officials, whom he called "bloodsuckers." Lebow had built the New York City Marathon on the backs of the elite runners, yet he had barely a nickel for them. Lebow groused about Rodgers's demands for appearance money, while he paid himself a handsome salary from entry fees and corporate sponsors. He stiffed city officials for most of the cost of shutting down roads and bridges, while the New York Road Runners bought a townhouse off Fifth Avenue. Now he was trying to get Rodgers to return to New York to face Salazar in front of a national television audience, knowing full well that Rodgers was not up to form and that Salazar would "pulverize" him. As Rodgers saw it, it was all part of Lebow's disrespect for the runner as an athlete and the triumph of carnival over sport.

Still, he might have done it if the money had been right. But Lebow, ever the tightwad, refused to accede to Rodgers's demands, which had increased more than tenfold since Lebow delivered $2,000 to him in a paper bag in 1976. Money concerns kept Rodgers out of Falmouth as well. Bowing to political pressure, Rich Sherman and John Carroll declined to offer runners any prize or appearance money. Instead, Rodgers accepted an invitation to run the Stockholm Marathon in Sweden, where they knew how to treat an amateur.

Salazar was happy to run Falmouth for a song. He wasn't immune to the lure of a bag o' cash, but he had his Nike contract and no divorce to support. Although he had no love for the officials who ran the sport — whom he called "young, stinking businessmen" — he was the product of a university system that had not only trained him but also supported him with time, scholarship money, and free medical treatment. Unlike Yale or Wesleyan, the University of Oregon was essentially a farm team for the running majors. Thus, unencumbered by Rodgers's need to earn a living or Shorter's professional obligations, Salazar could pick and choose his races. He agreed to run Falmouth because it had nearly killed him, and because there were some who suggested he was afraid to run. That was all the motivation he needed.

Call it overcompensation, then, for how he swaggered into town, predicting a new course record and declaring that he would run the race in under thirty-two minutes, a feat that had never been accomplished. Not only that, he said he would attempt to set a new U.S. ten-kilometer road race record. Once again, he didn't see his predictions as arrogance; they simply reflected a fair assessment of his abilities based on his fitness, prior experience, and recent races. He knew he was fast — faster than he had ever been — and in his current condition, the record didn't stand a chance. Another athlete might have qualified his statements, or might have recognized how he would be perceived and resorted to clichés about "respecting the course" and "giving 110 percent." But why bother? He wasn't contending for the Mr. Congeniality Award. In fact, his predictions gave him a competitive advantage, because only the foolhardy would try to catch him. By the time he stepped up to the starting line, he had already defeated most of his competitors in their own minds.

The towns of Falmouth and Woods Hole buzzed with Salazar fever. That summer, world events such as the birth of MTV, the retirement of Walter Cronkite, and the marriage of Prince Charles and Lady Di seemed inconsequential sideshows to the main event. Instead, the conversations on the beaches and in the supermarkets and cafés were all about whether Salazar would really run under thirty-two minutes. People who knew nothing about "jogging" found themselves debating the wisdom of setting an early pace versus holding back until the beach. The Red Sox were ignored while every skinny kid became a running expert. It was as if an entire sports-obsessed region had chucked out its gloves, bats, and balls for a pair of racing flats.

For a month, the *Falmouth Enterprise* published a steady stream of articles about the upcoming event — breathless reports about the family that was hosting the Irish national champion or the girl who planned to watch the race from six different vantage points (and her tricks for beating the traffic). A week before the race, the newspaper devoted nearly every page to the event and included a complete list of the 4,200 runners. Meanwhile, the national press corps descended on the Cape, with sports reporters from every major paper rubbing shoulders with the locals. The *Boston Globe* rented a helicopter to improve its view, as did ESPN, WBZ, and *Sports Illustrated.*

The hotels had no vacancies, and enterprising homeowners made extra cash by renting out rooms. A dinner reservation was practically an impossibility, and a parking space was as coveted as in Manhattan at Christmas. It was crazy, simply mad, and Tommy Leonard could not believe the party he had created. He hopped from bar to bar, welcoming friends wherever he went, accepting good wishes like the mother of the bride. He had never been happier.

The night before the race, Salazar slipped into the Captain Kidd restaurant for dinner with Molly and his family. The restaurant had renamed a dish in his honor — Sole Salazar — and of course he had to order it (or risk offending his sponsors, Bill and Maggie Crowley). During the meal, he was interrupted half a dozen times by diners who wanted his autograph, including by his waiter, who had brought his own race number for Salazar to sign. José Salazar was thrilled with the attention, but Alberto looked like he just wanted to go home. The autograph seekers were no better than the media, and both were unwelcome distractions from the goal at hand. Fame was something Alberto suffered, the way another man suffered gout or syphilis: unfortunate byproducts of his passion. He did it for his father, and because he had no real choice in the matter. But if he could take the money and run, he would.

Finally, his social obligations completed, Alberto retired with Molly and stewed about indignities, large and small. His father was so damned controlling and his mother so passive. Why had he agreed to come to the Cape with them in the first place? Eventually,

Molly calmed him down, and he slept a few hours without gnashing his teeth or moaning and groaning.

In the morning, a steady rain threatened to upend the careful preparations of the race organizers. Rich Sherman and John Carroll scurried about, worrying over drainage, beach access, and helicopter flight plans. But once again, the heavens smiled upon Falmouth, and the rain stopped right before race time. The runners were wet, but not unhappy, and they discarded their makeshift raincoats and hats in piles around the Marine Biological Laboratory parking lot.

Salazar was impervious to weather — hot, cold, rain, wind, he ran in all conditions. But a wet course would have made a record more difficult. Now, as he did some stretching at the starting line, Water Street was swept clear of puddles by race volunteers. He shared a few words with his toughest competitors — Rod Dixon, Craig Virgin, and Mike McLeod from Great Britain — and greeted former GBTC teammates such as Bob Hodge. In the pack that day was John Gregorek, a future Olympian and 3:51 miler at Georgetown University, and Sosthenes Bitok from Kenya, another future Olympian, who held nearly every middle- and long-distance record at the University of Richmond.

When the gun went off, however, it was all Salazar, all the time. He was in the lead pack of four after the first mile, which he clocked in 4:29, and he hit the second mile in 4:31. Virgin had beat him three weeks earlier in the 5000 meters, and he knew that Dixon and McLeod could outkick him, so he set a hard pace to break them early. Virgin faded first, fatigued from fighting a stomach bug over the past few weeks. Salazar threw in a surge as they came down the small hill before the three-mile mark and dropped Dixon, but McLeod stubbornly held on. Three more times along Surf Drive Salazar surged, and three more times McLeod matched him. At five miles, however, Salazar surged again, and this time McLeod could not stay with him.

Salazar powered past the marina and into Falmouth Heights,

widening his lead with every stride. He missed the ten-kilometer mark, but he was still on pace for a course record. The crowds were enormous, bigger than they had ever been, and they screamed his name as he crested the hill in front of the Brothers Four. Dixon had passed McLeod for second place, but no one was watching; all eyes were on Salazar.

He was thinking now only about the record. He didn't need to look at his watch; he could tell the time from the sound of the crowd and the announcer's voice booming over the PA system. "Alberto Salazar . . . Wayland, Mass. . . . Athletics West and former member Greater Boston Track Club . . ."

When he broke the tape, the clock read 31:55.6. He had smashed the record by twenty-four seconds and become the first man to finish Falmouth under thirty-two minutes. On a course previously owned by Frank Shorter and Bill Rodgers, Alberto Salazar was no longer the heir apparent. Undefeated in the marathon and unflappable down the stretch, he was now the king of the roads. As he accepted his trophy from Tommy Leonard, the gathered multitude genuflected before him. He looked out over the crowd, and it was good.

A few months later, he made another prediction. It was as brash and bold as his prediction at Falmouth. He would break the world record at the New York City Marathon. When he made good on his prediction, running the marathon in 2:08:13, those who had seen him at Falmouth were not surprised. He was at the top of his game, injury-free and capable of anything. He said he could run 2:06 or 2:05, and no one doubted it. He was only twenty-three, and the world waited.

Time, however, was not on his side.

Alberto Salazar checking for Dick Beardsley in the final yards
of the famous "Duel in the Sun" at Boston in 1982.

Associated Press

18

Boom's End (1982)

Falmouth was like the Academy Awards: you had to be there to
compete for the Oscar or at least to walk the red carpet.
— AMBY BURFOOT

SOME SAY THE RUNNING BOOM ended on July 20, 1984,
the day Jim Fixx went for a six-mile run and dropped dead
of a heart attack at the age of fifty-two. Others say it ended
on April 12, 1982, the day Salazar fought Dick Beardsley to the wire
in the Boston Marathon, taking no water on an unseasonably warm
day, after which he was rushed to the medical tent and given six liters
of saline solution intravenously. Some say the boom never ended, or
that we're living in a second boom, or that "boom" implies "bust,"
and because there was never the latter, there couldn't be the former.

But the truth is, the running boom ended on August 15, 1982.
That was the date on which Alberto Salazar broke the record again
at Falmouth, running 31:53.3 and beating Craig Virgin and Rod
Dixon on national television, with commentary provided by Frank
Shorter. Fixx's death was tragic but not entirely inexplicable. He had
been a heavy smoker and weighed 220 pounds before he took up

running. His own father had died of a heart attack at age forty-three. So while Fixx was considered a guru of the running boom whose death — to many people — signaled its end, in fact running probably added another decade to his life.

As for the "Duel in the Sun" — Salazar's battle with Beardsley at Boston — it was not the first time Alberto ran himself into the ground or needed medical treatment after a race. A few months after that race, he recovered well enough to set U.S. records in the 5000 and 10,000 meters. Shortly thereafter, he won Falmouth again, setting another course record. The marathon may have hurt him, but it didn't slow him down.

After August 15, 1982, however, Salazar began to wane. He won the New York City Marathon, but his time was more than a minute slower than the previous year's. A few months later, he ran his worst time in three years in a 10,000-meter race in Eugene. At the world track-and-field championships, he barely qualified for the finals in the event, then finished far back in the pack. His injuries recurred, and he suffered bouts of bronchitis. He finished second to Pete Pfitzinger at the U.S. Olympic marathon trials, and ended up in fifteenth place at the 1984 Los Angeles Olympics. In short, he was done.

Salazar's decline, however, was more than personal: it signified the decline of American male distance runners on the international scene. (Women's performances declined at the same rate, but the decline started a few years later, perhaps because their entrance into the boom also had started a few years later.) His course record at Falmouth stood for ten years until it was broken by a Kenyan, Benson Masya. Masya's win was the second victory by an African there in a string that, since 1991, reads like this: Kenya, Kenya, Kenya, Kenya, Kenya, Kenya, Morocco, Morocco, Kenya, Kenya, Kenya, Kenya, Kenya, Kenya, Kenya, Kenya, Kenya, Ethiopia, Ethiopia, Ethiopia, Kenya, Kenya.

Indeed, since Salazar's victories in 1982, only one American man has won Falmouth (Bruce Bickford in 1985) and no American-born man has won a marathon in New York City, Boston, Chicago, or Los Angeles, or any other major distance race. (Meb Keflezighi, who emigrated from Eritrea to the United States when he was thirteen, won New York in 2010.) No American-born male distance runner has been ranked first in any event, and none has taken home an Olympic gold medal. Only one American, Ryan Hall, has ever run faster than Salazar's marathon time of 2:08:13, and none has ever matched his course record at Falmouth.

But on that day at Falmouth in August 1982, Alberto Salazar was faster than he had ever been. The illnesses and injuries that would afflict him were still just nagging pains — barely noticeable occupational hazards. He had few equals, and he felt unbeatable. He already owned the world record in the marathon, and he aimed to add the 10,000 meters as well. "Right now I'm in the top three or four [in the world]," he told the Associated Press. "But the guys ahead of me are in their 30s, and they don't have the improvement ahead that I do."

He let University of Florida junior and future Olympian Keith Brantly set an early pace for the first two and a half miles. He hung back, biding his time and taking the measure of his stomach, which had been upset the night before. But when the race came down Oyster Pond Road, he moved onto Brantly's shoulder and then passed him. Just like that, he was in the lead. Fifty yards. One hundred yards. No one went with him. No one dared.

"There goes Alberto," said Frank Shorter. "It's his race now."

The sun beat down on the beach. A tailwind pushed at his back. The course opened and beckoned. One foot, then the other. The simplest of motions and yet the most complicated: balance, agility, foresight. His arms in sync with his breathing. His legs tuned true to the road. Head held high and eyes focused in front.

See him run.

From left to right: Mike Roche, Craig Virgin, Bill Rodgers, and Alberto Salazar duel for the lead along Surf Drive in the 1978 Falmouth Road Race.

Courtesy Bill Rodgers

Epilogue

I T'S BEEN THIRTY YEARS since Frank Shorter, Bill Rodgers, and Alberto Salazar ruled the roads. Today, more people run than ever before. At last count, there were forty million in the United States alone. Yet rather than spawning a new generation of champions, as it might in another sport, this phenomenal growth has slowed the median pace in the typical race. The average time in the marathon, for example, has gone from 3:32:17 in 1980 to 4:16:34 in 2011. It has also coincided with the decreasing competitiveness of U.S. runners.

Some of the slowing is explained by the increase in the number of women, who tend to run slower than men. But that is only part of the story. Even among the elite, there has been a significant decline in performance. Consider that in 1978, more than two thousand runners broke the magic three-hour barrier in the Boston Marathon. In 2012, with a field six times as large, only about five hundred runners broke three hours. At the Falmouth Road Race in 1982, a finishing time of thirty-six minutes was good enough for only eighty-ninth place. But in 2012, the same time would have earned a runner thirty-second place. Meanwhile, fewer than one-third of the men who qualified for the U.S. Olympic marathon trials in 2012 would have met the qualifying standard in 1984. At the 2000 Olympics, only one American met the Olympic standard, and he finished sixty-ninth. The story is the same at nearly every event along the distance ladder. With the exception of a few standouts, U.S. runners cannot match the times of their earlier progenitors and stand little chance on the international circuit.

What explains this fall from the heights, and why should we care?

In general, there has been a movement away from running as a sport where people run fast, to running as an activity done for fitness or social purposes. For this we can blame, in part, the people who cultivated the first running boom: the men whose enthusiasm for the sport drove millions to the roads. In popularizing running, they inadvertently dumbed it down, celebrating the participant over the winner. When Tommy Leonard called Falmouth a "moving street party," he unintentionally emphasized the beer drinking rather than the racing. When Fred Lebow moved the New York City Marathon to the streets of New York, he elevated the schlepper over the racer. The elite runners drew the masses to the roads, but once they were there, the elites were forgotten. Today it is common for finishers in a major race not to know — and not to care — who won. What counts is the personal narrative of adversity and achievement. There are no heroes; there are only goody bags and fancy flavored waters.

This shift is reflected in the media, which used to cover running as a sport but now treats it as a lifestyle event. Even publications dedicated to running have changed their emphasis from reporting on racing to providing tips on diet and fitness. Gone are the days when Joe Henderson, Derek Clayton, Kenny Moore, and Amby Burfoot — competitive runners all — wrote about who won, who lost, and how to get faster. Now we have articles about how to get six-pack abs and which exotic location to choose for a running vacation. No doubt the editors know their audience, but the audience is also influenced by the editors.

At the same time, it's not a coincidence that the public has embraced popular movements that are antithetical to speed. Barefoot

214

running, for example, may help indigenous Central American tribes hunt game, but it has never made anyone fast. (Even Abebe Bikila eventually bought himself a pair of shoes.) Meanwhile, "penguins" — runners so slow they waddle when they walk — celebrate finishing as if it were victory. Finally, we have New Age gurus such as Jeff Galloway — a former elite athlete who should know better — teaching that walking in the middle of a race will make runners faster. Their enthusiasm is admirable, but it won't bring home any medals.

Running can be brutal — terrible for the back and knees and hips and feet. Today, Bill Rodgers and Frank Shorter walk like men twenty years older, and Alberto Salazar suffered a heart attack in 2008 that he attributes to the damage done by racing. Their struggles with injury and illness have made running hard seem unpleasant, while the death of Jim Fixx punctured the myth that running could make a man immortal. As a result, fewer young athletes are attracted to the sport, especially when there are so many alternatives — not to mention video games.

Money has also played an important role in the decline of great American runners. At first, the lack of it — and the struggle over amateur rules — drove some talented athletes into other sports. Then, when it became available, it drove runners into the arms of agents and managers, who eschewed clubs such as the FTC and GBTC. Soon the vibrant culture where runners trained, drank, and raced together withered and died. Today many running clubs have trouble attracting serious athletes, while elite runners train on their own, with no one to push them except a watch and a coach.

But there is hope. For the first time in forty-eight years, two American distance runners won medals at the London Olympics in 2012. Galen Rupp took home the silver in the 10,000 meters, as did Leo Manzano in the 1500 meters. Rupp trains with Nike's Oregon Project, coached by Alberto Salazar, as does the United Kingdom's Mo Farah, who won the 5000 and 10,000 meters in London. The Oregon Project was established in part to capture the spirit of the running clubs that nurtured Shorter, Rodgers, and Salazar, as well as to provide a high-tech culture in which the next generation of stars can develop.

Today men such as Rupp, Manzano, and Ryan Hall (also coached by Salazar), and women such as Shalane Flanagan and Kara Goucher, are competing internationally with the best in the world. But there is a lot of ground to be made up. The first step is to create more initiatives like the Oregon Project to support more runners, and to offer more races to showcase their talents. To outsiders, running may seem like a lonely, isolating experience. But, in fact, it is teammates who make a runner better, stronger, and faster. Good luck also plays a role — the fortuity of the right men (and women) at the right time competing against one another to become the new king (or queen) of the roads.

In the end, running fast is not about fame or fortune. It's not even about winning. It's about pushing the human body to the limit, testing our endurance, finding the will to triumph when the black maw of defeat engulfs us. It's about staring at death and beating it back, kicking it hard to the other side of the road. *No, not today. I've got a race to run.*

Acknowledgments

This book could not have been written without the initial encouragement of Bruce Tracy and the gentle prodding of Laura Ford. Both understood how important running is to me, and both pushed me to explore it. I also owe a debt to Bruce Nichols at Houghton Mifflin Harcourt, who saved me when I thought the book was dead, and my editor, Susan Canavan, who helped me revive it. Thanks as well to Ashley Gilliam and Beth Burleigh Fuller at Houghton Mifflin Harcourt and copyeditor Barbara Jatkola. Finally, nothing I write goes anywhere without the critical eye of my agent, Lisa Bankoff, who breaks bad news gently and good news immediately, and has done so for eighteen(!) years.

I am very grateful for the time and memories freely given to me by John and Lucia Carroll, Tommy Leonard, and Rich and Kathy Sherman. John Brant, Arthur Crago, Ellen Cushman, Jim Gerweck, Jim Hansen, Jason Kehoe, Alex Shorter, and Louise Shorter were also very helpful. Amanda Wastrom and Charlie Rodgers found me some great photos, and Bob Hodge and Jack Bacheler provided me with unbeatable historical records. My research assistants, Caitlin Parker, Cara Giaimo, and Sean Doocy, made me smarter than I am, and both Caitlin and Cara conducted additional interviews and plumbed the library stacks for terrific nuggets.

Of course, there would be no book if not for the runners who shared their stories. Thanks to Nancy Robinson Alferes, Jack Bacheler, Amby Burfoot, Rudy Chapa, Bill Dellinger, Rod Dixon, Johanna Forman, Joe Henderson, Bob Hodge, Jack McDonald, John Parker, Kirk Pfrangle, Tammy Hennemuth Race, Mike Roche, Joan Benoit Samuelson, Bill Squires, Craig Virgin, and Grete Waitz. Bill Rodgers, Alberto Salazar, and Frank Shorter graciously sat still for all my questions and annoying follow-up e-mails. Most important, they were the source of inspiration — both then and now — for which I am deeply thankful.

Finally, I am very lucky to have a wonderful wife and two amazing children, which never was clearer to me than after one run that was almost my last. Thank you for being in my life.

Index

Note: Page references in *italics* refer to photographs.